THE BREAK-UP BIBLE

The Keep Strong,
Let Go and Move on Guide

Magda B. Brajer

THE BREAK-UP BIBLE

The Keep Strong, Let Go and Move on Guide

Magda B. Brajer

THE BREAK-UP BIBILE: Copyright © July, 28 2013

By: Magda B. Brajer

London -

All rights reserved. Printed in the United States of America. No part of this book may be used or reproduced in any manner whatsoever without written permission except in the case of brief quotations embodied in critical articles or reviews.

This book must not be reproduced in whole or in parts by any means, without permission. Making or distributing copies of this book constitutes infringement and could subject the infringer to criminal and civil liability.

This book contains the personal opinions of the author.

For more information contact:

Author email:
Speak_to_magda@hotmail.com

Or visit the author's website at:

www.magdabbrajer.com

ISBN-13: 978-1515249078

ISBN-10: 1515249077

First Edition for print by: Create Space, July 2013

DEDICATION

I would like to dedicate this book to my grandmothers, Urszula and Stefania, and to my great grandmother, Teodora.

CONTENTS

Welcome!	1
Part 1: Why No Contact Always Works	**5**
Ch. 1: So You Are Single	6
Ch. 2: The Basics Of The 'No Contact' Rule	9
Ch. 3: The Victim Of Circumstances	14
Ch. 4: Crime And Punishment	16
Part 2: Surviving The Break-Up From Hell	**19**
Ch. 5: How Do I Cope With My Broken Heart?	20
Ch. 6: 24 Hours To A Week After The Break-Up	21
Ch. 7: 2 To 6 Weeks After The Break-Up	26
Ch. 8: How To Stop Yourself Making A Panic Call	32
Ch. 9: The Internet Trap	37
Ch. 10: How To Act On Facebook And Twitter	39
Ch. 11: How To Emotionally Survive Looking Him Up On The Internet	43
Ch. 12: What You Absolutely Need To Know Before You Spy On Him On Facebook And Twitter	45
Ch. 13: When His Internet Life Becomes Too Much Too Handle	50
Ch. 14: 6-12 Weeks After The Break-Up	53
Ch. 15: What Exactly Is 'Warrior Mode'?	56
Ch. 16: 3-6 Months After The Break-Up	62
Part 3: Questions And Answers About Your Break-Up	**69**
Ch. 17: When Will He Realize You Have Stopped The Contact For Good And What It Does To Him?	70

Ch. 18: If I Want Him Back, Should I Be Seen With Other Men To Make Him Jealous? — 72
Ch. 19: What If I Meet Someone I Really Like? — 74
Ch. 20: Can I Have A 'Friends With Benefits' Relationship With Another Man If I Want My Ex Back? — 77
Ch. 21: Should I Stay Friends With My Ex? — 80
Ch. 22: If We Are Meant To Be Together, How Long Will It Take For Him To Call Me? — 84
Ch. 23: What You Gained By Separating From Him — 87
Ch. 24: What He Lost By Separating From You — 92

Part 4: Getting Back Together — **95**
Ch. 25: How To React To A Text Or Email From Him — 96
Ch. 26: How To Handle The First Phone Call From Him — 104
Ch. 27: How To Act When You Meet Him For The First Time Since The Break-Up — 109

Part 5: Not Getting Back Together — **122**
Ch. 28: Understanding Why He Still Hasn't Called — 123
Ch. 29: How To Handle The News That Your Ex Started Dating — 134

Part 6: Learning From Your Break-Up — **145**
Ch. 30: If Men Love Sweethearts, Why Do They Marry Bitches? — 146
Ch. 31: How To Get Respect From A Future Partner — 154
Ch. 32: Why Are We Masochists? — 157
Ch. 33: If It Sounds Too Good To Be True It Probably Is! — 159
Ch. 34: Your Online Presence Going Forward — 164

Part 7: The End Of This Book, The Beginning Of The Brand New You! — **167**
Ch. 35: Last Few Words From Magda — 168
Ch. 36: How To Get The Guy: Capture The Heart Of Mr Right — 171
Other books by Magda B Brajer — 173

WELCOME!

THANK GOD FOR YOUR EX... WITHOUT HIM, YOU WOULDN'T BE READING THIS BOOK – A NOTE FROM THE AUTHOR

Hello again and thank you for choosing this book. I'm Magda, the author of *It Really Is All His Fault*, and of course, the book that is right in front of you.

Almost two years ago I found myself in the very same place you might be in today. Freshly single and devastated after the break-up with a man who was supposed to be that 'one and only', I searched high and low for answers on how to shake off the heartache and get hold of a magic eraser that would get him out of my head fast. I read books, I read online advice and I read blogs. The advice given to me by those sources made sense; it made perfect sense. It was whole-hearted and straight forward.

But somehow, even when I knew what the right thing to do was: not to call him; not to look him up on the internet; not to idealize him, it still failed to get me to live by that knowledge and incorporate it into my life. Why do I think this was the case? Well, one of the answers to this question lies within the phenomenon of human nature itself; we are always inclined to try for ourselves what we would advise others to not to do. Furthermore, the more help we get, the more we pull the other way. For me, this was no different.

If I read that it was bad for me to look my ex up on Facebook, I would perfectly agree, but couldn't quite shake off the compulsion to do it anyway. If I was told to stick to my plan and not text him, I would still do it, which for most of the time, only inflamed the situation. Even when I fully felt and realized the extent of the agonizing pain I was causing myself by bringing it all back this way, I would go back for more. Perhaps you do just that? How can I convince you that this book will heal you? How is this book different to anything you have read before?

My dear reader, the only thing I will say to you at this point is that this book will never just tell you what to do. It will explain and lead you, so you can make your own sense of it and ultimately, make your own decisions. And because you are an intelligent person with a lot of common sense, all you actually need is to understand something before you make a judgment on it or decide to apply it to your life. When you truly understand something, you don't just copy it for the sake of it, because even if you did, it wouldn't last. Instead you are making a conscious decision to apply it to your life. You are changing the way you think, and when you do that your perception on a situation, person or even yourself changes. Sometimes we need to take a step back in life to see what's right in front of us, and to appreciate that very often, the only difficulty in finding the best solution to the problem lies in us.

So, if you decided to buy this book, you no doubt need help to overcome the emotions accompanying the break-up of your previous relationship and getting over your ex 'leading man'. May the Oscar go to him – for the un-supporting role he played in your life. If he walked out on you and left you feeling an emotional wreck, I wish with all my heart that you turn the tables on him. And know that you have the power to make that happen! I want you to know that by buying this book you have taken a step forward and into your future, where you'll have choices to make about yourself and your new relationships. This book contains all the knowledge you need to arm yourself with the tools required to go out there and venture into new things and meet new people, including your new leading man. And even if that leading man is the same man that you are still are crying over today, know that by the sweet time he comes back to you, you will be the one holding all the cards, so ultimately you will have a new relationship and… a new partner.

It really is all about you! By buying this book you have made a choice to improve your life, and only wise people can identify the need to 'do something about something' in the first place. I feel proud and privileged that you are about to start that journey here and now. I have taken it myself. Some might say I am still on it. But when your destination is happiness, you drive to it every day. Another thing about human nature is that we are hugely greedy. So I wish you the greatest greed in the world when it comes to your own happiness. I hope you'll get to eat all the pies!

Magda

PART 1

WHY NO CONTACT ALWAYS WORKS – THE BEGINNING OF THE 'MOVING ON' JOURNEY

CHAPTER 1

SO YOU ARE SINGLE

So, it has happened. You are newly single. It has either been on the cards for a while, or has completely taken you by surprise. The fact is what you now have to endure is the dreaded post-break-up heartache. It doesn't matter how many you've been through in the past, because even advanced experience in this area can't help to fight off the pain more quickly. Besides, as we grow older and endure yet another break-up, it might just be even harder to deal with it. On top of the usual heartbreak, you come to a realization that this was yet another relationship that did not work out.

Regardless of whether he was a bastard or not, whether he dumped you, or his behavior forced you to dump him, and whether you do or don't want him back, almost every break-up is accompanied by feelings of frustration, anger, humiliation and grief. Most are also accompanied by the feeling of wanting revenge. Most men don't have to humiliate you by cheating for you to want revenge. They may have just treated you badly, not shown you attention or refused to emotionally open up or take the relationship to another level, and that is humiliating enough.

I would like to stipulate at this point that if you do decide that making him regret breaking up with you involves any behavior of a malicious or violent nature, this book is not for you. Revenge, if executed this way, becomes a wasted and painful emotion to endure, and it will only justify that he was right to be as far away from you as possible. Classy women do not take physical revenge on their exes. They don't treat their cars to key scratches, don't bad-mouth them to their friends and remain dignified on social media sites.

Most of us feel that we need to grovel, beg and ask for forgiveness immediately after the break-up, even if we haven't done anything wrong. I have taken this route before. Trust me, it's not pretty. I knew damn well that my ex was the one who should beg my forgiveness, but I was so hooked on continuing to see him, I thought I ought to do that in order to make us right. Well, I was *wrong*! He did agree to continue our relationship, but from then on he held all the cards. And of course, from the very moment he took me back, I felt enormous resentment that I'd had to beg, which led to streams of arguments. We lasted just another three months.

Today I know that even after you've groveled, begged and embarrassed yourself, there is a very simple way to get your power back. The first step is to STOP CONTACTING HIM! *RIGHT NOW!*

CHAPTER 2

THE BASICS OF THE 'NO CONTACT' RULE

Like many women who feel desperate to keep their relationships, I have done the unthinkable and begged for him to share his feelings. But instead of giving you details of these pathetic encounters, I am going to tell you how it ended. One day, and after many (empty) threats that I was going to leave, I called my ex to have a morning chat. There was nothing unusual about my phone call, but for reasons only known to him, from the very moment he picked up the call he was pissed off I was in his ear. Sure, when I used to call, his usual substitute for "Hello" was: "Can I call you later?" And I would always say: "Yes, sure," because I knew he'd be at work and might be busy.

However, it's funny how it plays on your mind and makes you a little insecure, because you never seem to be the person who he actually looks forward to talking to. Anyway, that morning, despite being abrupt, he didn't waste a single second of his time to reassure me that everything was okay, and when he called back several hours later, he proceeded to create an argument in which he called me needy and desperate. He demanded to know why I felt the need to call him, like it was unusual or out of character for me to do so. I don't remember the rest of the call. The only thing I knew was that his words hurt, *really* hurt.

Was this exactly what I needed to finally get that he was dragging me down emotionally and physically – and was in other words – no good for me? I didn't insist on continuing the conversation, and from what I can remember, it quickly finished. But the following morning he called again - with a slightly different attitude. He appeared to sound slightly 'sheepish', but as always, full of himself. To make matters worse, he denied what he had said the day before. Although it was frustrating, I was used to it, because it wasn't uncommon for him to take back his words and proclaim that I'd imagined everything. This is not uncommon - emotional wimps like him believe their own lies.

There was something different in my attitude though; I started questioning myself about exactly how much more humiliation I had to endure for the sake of this relationship. It was safe to say that no other man had ever treated me like this before, and I had no idea how to deal with it. So there it was, the slowly growing, yet powerful feeling that this time, enough was really enough, and he had, in fact overestimated his capacity to keep me hanging on. I finished it there and then, and I never called or spoke to him again. But I would love to see, for the sake of my own entertainment, how he waited for my calls since then, and the shock he got after weeks went by and I still hadn't got in touch. Instead, I went to America and self-published my first book, while he UNDOUBTEDLY sat and waited for any form of contact from me. I didn't need anyone to tell me this was the case, or confirm to me that it was happening, I just knew, and I didn't have any reason to doubt my intuition. He took me for granted and paid the price; the roles had reversed!

Great news: the chances are your ex will be feeling exactly the same! But the first thing you have to do to make this happen is to STOP CONTACTING HIM RIGHT NOW! This book will teach you, without playing any games, to reach the mode in which you are able to put yourself first, and he won't be able to break you emotionally anymore. And that's really all you need to stay strong. When you apply this powerful knowledge, you might just force him to look at you in a different light and reconsider his decision. You will effortlessly make him regret losing you, and make him realize that you were the best thing that ever happened to him. More importantly, you will be able to help him look back at his past behaviors and finally acknowledge the mistakes he made and take responsibility. You will then gain his respect. At the very least you will become the woman who got away with her head held high - and that's of course a far more remarkable an exit than the tearful doormat who cried for his attention and then went back for more.

No one knows what the future holds. Right now, because you are hurting, you may want reassurance that you will get back together with him and be blissfully happy. And no matter what circumstances surrounded your break-up, sometimes you will, but first you have to learn to regain the power and maintain it. Imagine yourself driving a car and breaking down. There nothing you can do. You have to patiently wait for the recovery services. They say 'patience is a virtue', and it is one of the wisest things ever spoken. In this case, by learning to be patient, you will allow your ex to understand what has happened from your point of view, and slowly make him want to become the 'recovery services'. But you need to let him learn the hard way and have no mercy. In other words, you have to take a massive step back. Just imagine the shock he will experience when you do just that. He may have told you that you are too intense, or may have found other faults in you to use as an excuse to finish the relationship. But it may have not have registered with you previously, and you continued to make the same mistakes. Even if he has left you to date another woman, trust me, as you make absolutely no effort whatsoever to contact him, he will slowly start to question *why he left you in the first place*, and will start remembering only the positive aspects of the relationship.

You may ask me at this point: "If I don't stay in contact with him, we obviously won't be talking about this, so how will I really know?" To which my reply is: trust your intuition girl, you know exactly how he will be feeling and what his reaction will be – *because you know him!* So let him wallow in self-pity! He may have told *you* before to stop feeling sorry for *yourself*. He might have been smug and arrogant, and yes, he thought he was being clever. But make no mistake, the moment you cut him out, you will force him to *taste his own medicine* - but that's just the beginning!

CHAPTER 3

THE VICTIM OF CIRCUMSTANCES

If at this point of your life, you are going through a break-up, I can only assume that things weren't right between the two of you for some time. Maybe prior to what happened, you spent hours asking yourself if he really loved you? Have you ever questioned his love, passion, attention, intentions and commitment? Did it make you feel insecure, even if you never considered yourself an insecure person before? He may have even blamed you for pushing him away because you became too needy and looked for his attention too often.

If you can answer "Yes" to some of these questions, it is safe to say you were the victim of circumstances that he created. Yet, of course, he was unable to see that, because he never wondered whether he was doing enough for you to feel happy and secure. And why? Because he didn't have to fight for you - as you always seemed satisfied with whatever he decided to give you. But now you have stopped all contact with him, it is easier for him to finally understand how that felt, because by reversing your behavior you are reversing the roles, and therefore transferring all those feelings onto him. And while he is starting to feel insecure, he will also start to question whether you ever truly loved him. I know, this may seem ridiculous, but it's true. This is what rejection does to people!

Don't think for a second that you ought to provide him with quick answers to anything. Allowing him to ask these burning questions of himself, and dwelling on the sudden insecurity he feels, is much needed, as it is the first step in making him understand how you felt and what made you act the way you did. In order to make him regret the break-up and regret letting go of you, you must allow him to feel deeply rejected and heartbroken. And by not contacting him you are actually rejecting him, because you're not acknowledging his existence in your life anymore. Don't fear that he will forget you in a hurry, or develop feelings of resentment because you are ignoring him. If he truly loves you he will be beating himself up for behaving badly towards you and for not appreciating you. *Total silence* is a crucial step you have to take to make him understand things from your point of view. Without which he will never, ever feel remorse, understand you or miss you.

CHAPTER 4

CRIME AND PUNISHMENT

Between the age of two and four, my great-grandmother, Teodora, looked after me full-time, as my parents and remaining grandparents were working or busy with other arrangements. To this day I remember one particular morning I spent with her as a three-year-old child. That morning I refused to eat my breakfast. Teo didn't plead or reason with me, instead she quietly informed me: "Lunch is at 1:00pm." Then she got up, took my food from the table and dropped it in the waste bin. Needless to say in a very short space of time I was getting hungry, and I started asking her to make me some food. She stayed in her rocking chair, continued knitting my scarf and remained unresponsive. That day I had to wait with a rumbling belly for my lunch to arrive, and it didn't come a minute earlier than she said it would. As far as I can remember, I even licked my plate clean!

When I think about that early memory of the two of us that day, there is never a time I don't smile to myself and admire what a great influence she was, and how she truly cared for me. She wanted me to learn something from that experience, so she did not just give in to me for the sake of her own peace of mind. In one single morning she had taught me that in life we always have to face the consequences of our actions.

But leaving my great grandmother and that breakfast behind, just think: why should your ex be spared the consequences of his actions? If you provide him with the luxury of your presence in his life or continuous contact, he will never miss you or learn where and how he went wrong; he will never understand he hurt you. By acting this way, too many women allow men to think they are somehow special, when this is not the case. The only thing that transpires from such behavior is the weakness of us women, and that putting up with crappy behavior from men makes them walk all over us.

I can see only now, after all this time, that I have a different perspective about my ex; the man I was desperate to remain in a relationship with. I can see that he is very average, dull, lacks guts and feeds off other people's ideas - to name a few observations. And I don't want a man who is any of these things, let alone all of them! The point I'm trying to make is, I would never be able to recognize any of this if I'd continued to stay in contact with him. So, *do not* call, text, tweet, email or Facebook message your ex, because he MUST endure what your absence in his life means if you want him to respect you or want you back. Furthermore, you must allow yourself to discover things from an unemotional perspective, and that only comes with time. When you get there you may find, like myself, that you don't want anything to do with a man you thought you so desperately wanted. And when you are hurting from the breakdown of a relationship, there is nothing better to help you get over him for good.

So, how do you get there…?

PART 2

SURVIVING THE BREAK-UP FROM HELL

CHAPTER 5

HOW DO I COPE WITH MY BROKEN HEART AFTER THE BREAK-UP?

As much as everyone else tells you that the break-up with your ex happened for the best, and you are better off without him, we both know it does not automatically heal your broken heart and help you forget about him. It does not help you to deal with the whole variety of emotions you are experiencing either. I understand if right now you feel like you have been placed in a big black hole and there is no way out of it. I also know that sometimes our friends' good advice simply does not work. Perhaps you feel like this nightmare will never end and you will never get over what has happened. But trust me on this, if I did it, so can you, so repeat after me: "I WILL GET THROUGH IT!"

CHAPTER 6

24 HOURS TO A WEEK AFTER THE BREAK-UP

It has been just hours since he cruelly left you. If you suspected that things had not been right for weeks or even months, your intuition was proven right. If you have ever experienced the death of someone close, you will know that when a serious relationship ends it feels exactly the same; like someone died; something has ended. It's over and it may be for good, hence the emotions. The first thing you experience is shock. The second is denial. Because these two powerful emotions grab hold of you it is extremely difficult to maintain balance between getting mad and staying dignified. All rational thought flies out of the window. But then all the emotions you are experiencing are conflicting: you hate him but you still love him; you resent him but you want him to fix this; you don't want him anywhere near you but you just want him to hold you; you want him to take back his words but you want to make him suffer like he made you suffer.

In moments of clarity, your first instinct is to repair or recover what was lost. So what do you do? You go into 'recovery mode' and try to fix something that (right now) can't be fixed, because he doesn't want it to be fixed. Recovery mode includes begging, groveling, shouting and/or promising you will change, even if you have not actually done anything wrong. As he refuses to cooperate, you go into the 'resentment mode', which can include, but not exclusively, screaming, insulting him and/or saying things you actually don't mean. During this time you stay in contact with him, because you are probably looking for some sort of closure, but unfortunately you will not find that now. This is the reality: you have to, absolutely *have to*, break all contact with him, *all contact*. I know it's hard, and no matter what I say to you right now, your instinct will be telling you that you should call him and fight for what's left, put together what has just been broken. But you are only inflaming the situation. Even if you call him without any desire to argue, and want to talk things through calmly and in a reasonable manner, he, or the manner he will speak to you, might provoke you to lose your temper and then you'll only reinforce in his head that he's right to be shot of you - because you are unstable. I know it really is all his fault, and you'll know it was never your intention to start another argument, but it will happen. Guaranteed! The more you push, the more he'll swing the other way. Leave him to it! Let him have his way! Disappear from his life. He will notice the silence and he will notice one more thing: he does not like that silence as much as he thought he would. Guaranteed.

At this early stage of the break-up you are just getting over the shock of it, and may still be in denial that any moment your ex will change his mind and dramatically walk back into your life. Miracles happen and it might sometimes be the case, but for now it is highly unlikely; you have to forget about it. However, if it really was to happen - don't just welcome him with open arms! Remember his crime? Don't spare him his punishment!

As much as your heart is breaking, you have to take steps to keep your mind occupied so you don't spend all your days and nights thinking about him. If you are not sleeping well or can't sleep at all, do take herbal remedies and try hypnosis. You will be surprised how well they work. If you can't eat properly, do try to make sure, even if you eat just once a day, that it is good food rather than junk. Look after yourself and try not to drink alcohol and *do not* take drugs. These things are not remedies for anything.

I have met many people who got addicted to alcohol or drugs while they were going through a traumatic time in their lives, so do keep that in mind. I know it is the least desirable time for you to think about your looks and beauty regime, but you are still appearing in public, so make at least the minimum effort at this stage – you owe it to yourself. If you can't face people at work or you are simply unable to concentrate on your duties, talk to your boss. Some work places are friendlier than others, but just remember that you are going through a bereavement, so if you are strong enough to have an open and honest conversation with your boss, do present it that way. If you can't take time off, book a holiday at short notice. I don't mean leave the country literally, unless you can - I mean book time off work to recuperate. Even if you think you have wasted this precious time off, time you could have spend somewhere hot, remember that you do need this time to recover, whatever you end up doing. If you miss out on this year's holiday abroad, don't worry, you can take that opportunity next year. Right now you need to get yourself together.

When I say you need time to yourself, I certainly don't mean that you shut yourself at home and cry yourself to sleep every lonely night. This is a crucial time for you to use the support of friends, but remember you have to be respectful and accommodating of the fact they have their own lives and problems. Do pour out your heart to them, you don't need to be analytical or constructive, you are not seeing a therapist, but a friend. You can cry on your best friend's sleeve all night long, just as long as she or he is still fine to go to work the next day.

When I was in this phase of my break-up, all advice I read in books and online said: "Enroll on some course, join a discussion group or a panel, learn new skills". All this sounds fantastic, but it might be spoken by a person who is not going through a break-up right now, or has forgotten how it feels. But I don't think these are good moves at this stage. I certainly wasn't ready to go out and face meeting new people just then. My mind was most certainly not focused on learning a foreign language or doing a knitting course! Besides, I think this could be potentially damaging to your already shattered self-esteem. If you force yourself to go and do something out of your comfort zone, you might realize halfway through that you can't handle it. Imagine the embarrassment of leaving a class-full of people, for example, because you can't stand to be there for a second longer. The right time to engage in such activities will come later.

Most importantly, during this stage you must make a clean break from him. No more phone calls, text messages and emails. No more social media. Remember, if you are serious about getting over him, getting him back, or making him regret losing you, you can't achieve any of the above if you don't stop contacting him!

CHAPTER 7

2 TO 6 WEEKS AFTER THE BREAK-UP

Now that you have become silent and you no longer act on impulse to call him, you need to start looking for real (not temporary) support to help you get your life back in order. Friends and family are still massively important at this stage, but you need to start dealing with your feelings without the need to process EVERYTHING with your close ones. This is the stage where you are regaining your emotional independence and starting to deal with most of your emotions on your own.

During this time, you stop feeling shock. You have now got used to the fact that you are not with him anymore. What you will be experiencing more and more of though, are anger and resentment towards him. You are now realizing how good you were to him, how well you treated him and how much his happiness was always your priority. You will be reliving specific examples of situations where you so badly wanted to show him that you were the perfect girlfriend. Perhaps you did things that he did not even know about? Were you waiting up half the night for his phone call? Were you waking up at 6:00am, while he was still sleeping, to put your make-up on so you could be the girlfriend he could be proud of? Did you spend countless hours cooking for him, supporting him, cleaning his house and other things that he never really noticed or took for granted? Even if you did these things out of your own initiative, you will be experiencing sadness and resentment because you'll be re-living his ungratefulness, and cursing yourself for being too available. Subsequently, if you made other mistakes, like being *too* attentive, now is the time to realize them. Perhaps you were stubborn and didn't acknowledge certain things about yourself, and only now have you realized that when he was trying to tell you something, he was actually right and you were resentful because you were just trying to work against him. Take stock and learn from this. It is empowering that us women *can* take responsibility for our actions. At least you know now you won't make those mistakes again. Maybe he can't act in the same way by going forward, so consider how much stronger than him that actually makes you.

During this stage you might also feel sorry for yourself. I know you don't want to continue feeling this way for a long time, but you need to, if only for a while. You might just come to a much needed and welcome conclusion that perhaps it doesn't pay to be too good to someone. Learn from that relationship and don't give another man the same benefits and privileges if you are not getting them in return. Imagine yourself as someone else, or in other words think of yourself in the third person, and how bad you would feel for a person in your situation. Draw comparisons.

However, when you are done feeling sorry for yourself you will unexpectedly experience a little wave of empowerment. This is when you will feel brave enough to confront belongings of his left in your place, or look through stuff you got from him. Be careful here though, because if you approach things too quickly, you will regret it later. During this time I threw away a few presents my ex bought me from his trip to India. I never really liked them, but I always appreciated the gesture. When my empowerment wave ended I did regret doing so because they were the only gifts he ever gave me.

Many women still don't understand that loving someone, even in the most healthy of ways, is a bit of an addiction in itself. We get addicted to that person because he is in our life, our thoughts, mind, dreams, future plans in messages on our phones, emails on our computer, etc, non-stop prior to the break-up. Cutting yourself off completely from every single memory of him and an object that represented him, when it might simply be too soon to do so, is not healing. You've already cut all contact, but it doesn't mean that you no longer remember your life with him, or that you have to do something that you are not ready for. That will only prolong or resurrect the feeling of the initial shock of the break-up.

Go gently on removing his belongings from your apartment and life. Cooperate with your own feeling of letting go. Get rid of one thing at the time and only when you're ready. Don't do that when your heart is still breaking and you are desperately yearning for his touch and the sound of his voice, etc, it will only upset you further. I have known women to throw out everything that reminded them of their exes, only to later break the no-contact rule because they were missing them so desperately. Know that in his absence, and in the absence of any form of contact from him, his T- shirt will do you much better than calling him. He will never know that you slept wearing it! However, if you do call him, it's a different thing all together. You will then have just revealed that you are still thinking about him and that you miss him. When he doesn't hear from you it intensifies his feelings of uneasiness, because he won't know what you are doing or thinking; men fall in love with women when they seem to be unavailable. Just one text message or phone call will let him know that you are thinking of him and that will put his mind at ease again. And a mind at ease means he no longer has to try to work out his part in the break-up. If your friends are pressuring you to get rid of his stuff, stand your ground and tell them you are not ready and you will at the right time for you.

During this time you should prepare for the highs, followed by the lows. The highs will empower you and the lows will crush you. *Live through it.* Don't try to escape reality. Don't drink to forget him or to feel any less hurt. You can't numb the pain forever, so if you want to get out of this black hole sooner rather than later, you'll need to face these emotions head-on; never run away from them.

As I mentioned before, at this stage you will be feeling growing resentment towards him, while still loving him. While it is perfectly natural to experience these conflicting feelings, because you have been betrayed by him, (even he did not cheat on you, he has still broken your heart), *it is more crucial than at any other stage that you still do not contact him!* Protect yourself as much as you can from acting on impulse and calling him. Sometimes all it can take is one bad memory, one reminder of his gutless behavior and you are there, furiously dialing his number. DON'T DO IT!

He doesn't have a clue what is going through your mind. He will never be drawn back to you if he hears your angry voice shouting in his ear a few weeks after the break-up. At this stage it could be double the damage, because if he has already started regretting the break-up, or is even just questioning himself as to why he decided to split up with you,

you would give him the easiest answer in the world: you are unstable. Not to mention that you would, again, reinforce that he was right to leave you in the first place.

Control the sudden urge to call him like you would control a panic attack. Not many people know that stopping a panic attack is actually very simple. All you have to do is stop the emergency message from being sent to your adrenal glands. You CAN calm yourself down by applying *four simple rules*. By drawing comparisons between a panic attack and a sudden angry urge to call your ex, I established that these rules are in fact a perfect way of stopping yourself from making the fatal mistake of calling him.

CHAPTER 8

HOW TO STOP YOURSELF MAKING A PANIC CALL TO YOUR EX

Firstly: calm down

The first thing you need to take control of is your breathing. Taking deep, regular breaths when you are upset will not only help you overcome your anger but also reduce your blood pressure, relax your muscles and reassure your body that you are 'safe', which in return will send that message to your thoughts. Breathe deeply through your nose filling your lungs, expanding your abdomen and breathe out through your mouth. In just a few minutes, you will experience a dramatic change in your behavior. Then take the opportunity to think how well you have done by not calling him, and how damaging it would be to do that right now. Reaching this point is crucial. If you calm yourself down now, you have already talked yourself out of calling him by 50 per cent.

Secondly: don't think in a negative way

You need to know that this fleeing moment of wanting to call him and get stuff off your chest, is just an emotion you've experienced. Medically speaking, this situation has raised your blood pressure and increased the level of adrenaline in your adrenal glands. You need to know that when you manage to calm yourself down it will pass. You may than experience another powerful set of emotions, you may cry and feel sorry for yourself for a moment, but trust me, it will all come to pass relatively quickly. Consider that you are not the first or the last person in the world going through a break-up, and realize that you are on the right track to get through it. Think how much anxiety you are giving him right now; buckets! And while you are still far from okay, you have to remember that HE DOES NOT KNOW THIS or any other information about you, and that's driving him insane. And this is the man who only few weeks ago kept hanging up on you and didn't want to know you! Are you proud of yourself for putting him in his place? You should be, girl, because you are doing amazingly well so far!

Thirdly: use coping statements

These are positive statements that are stronger than the catastrophic statements you have been torturing yourself with. Replace the negative thoughts with positive ones. Choose something that addresses those negative thoughts and crushes them.

When you are going through a moment of rage and want to make that disastrous phone call, you can calm yourself down by thinking the *opposite* of what's brought you to feel this way. So simple, yet not many women use this technique. One of the biggest reasons we feel anger and resentment towards a man after a break-up is the fact that he won't accept any responsibility for the pain he has caused us. So, for example, instead of calling him and, once again, shouting it in his ear, think of how, because of the actions you are taking right now, he will soon have to come to grips with the fact that he might have lost you for good and what that will do to him. Imagine that this anxiety will lead him further into questioning his behavior and you will soon find that without any nagging or contact, he will start realizing the things he was responsible for. *You just need to place that thought in your head instead of the initial destructive one.*

If your ex has left you to be with another woman, think that it's perhaps because he had commitment problems and was scared of the emerging closeness in your relationship. Consider then that his new relationship might not last very long either! Another example of replacing negative thought is: "Oh my God, I can't believe I will never see him again!" Replace that with: "I will be seeing him sooner than I could ever realize, I just have to stick to what I am doing right now!" THAT'S HOW IT WORKS!

If you have been through this at least once and have managed to calm yourself down and not give in, well done, I congratulate you. To remain cool when your blood is boiling is not an easy thing to do, but you managed it; you are a winner!

However, if you gave in to your emotions, perhaps it's time to work on your 'inner-winner' skills and prepare a list of coping statements in advance. Brainstorm the fearful thoughts that bring on your anxiety and anger and then make a long list of coping statements that you can look at when you need to, rather than trying to do that in the middle of the attack. I can't tell you enough how powerful and wonderful this tool really is. When I felt that rage growing inside me, I would always use my pre-prepared statements. It's what got me through my break-up with my head held high.

Fourthly: accept your feelings

When you consider that you are dealing with the matters of your heart, matters that cannot always be easily explained or solved, you need to at one stage or another recognize and accept your feelings, even if you can't yet deal with them. The first thing you need to achieve to recover from anything is acceptance. So, when you are overwhelmed by anger, rage or simply by sadness because he is no longer part of your life, you need to *accept what is*. You need to also accept that in that particular moment you just feel the way you feel. But whatever it is that you feel will pass! Don't give in to it! Wait it out. You will be glad you did.

CHAPTER 9

THE INTERNET TRAP

What makes getting over an ex partner so painful, is the fact that these days you can't forget about him in a hurry. Because even if you are not in contact with him, you may be surrounded by images of him and the news of his current life. In this modern world, our exes can't just disappear from our radar even if we, or they, were to move halfway across the world. We have communication now in the form of the internet and social networking sites that removes the choice of anyone moving anywhere to get away; there are no boundaries to communication.

Imagine that as little as ten years ago, when you broke up with someone, unless you had children with them, worked together or lived in the same neighborhood, the chances of seeing them again or finding out details of what they'd got up to after the break-up were pretty slim. But that was ten years ago. And it is rather scary to think that within such a short period of time we have willingly volunteered our privacy, instead allowing ourselves to be brutally invaded. The stories of our lives are now available on the internet for anyone to look up, this is a frightening fact, yet it is true.

A few years ago, the only women who had to endure publically seeing their exes in the arms of other women, or simply looking at their exes after the break up, were famous actresses and celebrities, whose lives were plastered all over the papers. Since 2006, when Marc Zuckerberg launched Facebook, we have the same 'privilege' as they do. The difference is, after the split, the rich and famous have the resources of being able to afford professional therapy, security, holidays out of the country and endless PR. You and I, however, don't have such advantages. When you spot his latest picture on the internet, regardless of the fact he is alone or with another woman, you are left to deal with it all on your own. And the details of his newly single, everyday life and what he's getting up to can be painful to endure – because you are no longer part of it.

CHAPTER 10

HOW TO ACT ON FACEBOOK AND TWITTER AFTER THE BREAK-UP

Going through my own break-up, I found myself surrounded with some advice that seemed right and straightforward, but unfortunately useless in practice. It was mainly to do with handling the split on the internet. Anyone can say that we should not look up our ex on social networking sites after the break-up, but does it actually stop anyone? Truth is, sooner or later, you will undoubtedly find yourself looking at him online. Of course the hard bit is, how to take in and digest the new dose of information about him generated from your computer? If you don't know the answer to that, I understand, and I am going to try to help you, because I know that you are missing him like crazy AND I don't want you to break the no contact rule.

The knowledge that I am going to share with you in the next few pages is straight- forward and realistic, it is advice on how to react when finding out about his newly single life without you.

Immediately after the break-up took place:

Let's start with Facebook. If your status on Facebook says: 'In a relationship' with so and so (your ex), you should change it at the first possibility. However, don't change it to 'Single', although effectively that's what you are, just leave it blank. Your break-up with him does not deserve to be awarded with special announcements to others. *Go back to basics*: no one needs to read your status updates, they are limited to few silly options anyway! They do not mean anything in real life. People feed off new, daily gossip, and you don't owe anyone any juicy info about your life! Comprende?

If you have few hundred friends, consider that this is not actually the number of real friends you have. Your true friends are the people who are helping you through it, they will find out about your break-up from you and don't need any other way but face-to-face to discuss it. Consider the amount of 'frenemies' you are harboring there (in your account). Are they there just so you can occasionally piss them off with a piece of great information about yourself that will make them explode with jealousy? Do you really want them to know that you are crushed by something as hard as a break-up? Ask yourself if, at this devastating moment, you can actually handle answering questions about your break-up, because throwing 'Single' out there will no doubt land you with endless messages about what happened. Beware of discussing what has happened with just anyone who approaches you (on the internet and in reality for that matter). I can only imagine that most people you know have links to your ex, and the last thing you want is for them to report back to him how devastated you really are! *Go back to basics*: leave your status blank, that way you are drawing less attention to it.

I can only presume that your ex was, or still is, a Facebook friend. And unless he un-friends you first, there is no need to un-friend him immediately after the break-up. You may ask me at this point, "What does this achieve?" And my answer would be: there is a certain nonchalance in the fact that immediately after the break-up you did not rush to remove him from your list of friends, and it also proves that any form of dealing with him no longer maintains the status of priority in your life. By acting this way you are letting everyone, him included, know that you are not sad and devastated about the break-up (even if it's not true and you just want to make it seem that way). It sends the right message. Is he still your partner? No. Will he be your friend? No. Will he be begging you to get back together with him? Perhaps. So you might as well portray the right break-up image from the beginning. Important question: how long do you keep him as a friend on your social networking site? The answer is few days to a couple of weeks. If he has removed you before that, you don't have to worry about it. You also don't have to worry about looking desperate because you didn't do it first. Trust me, the "I haven't got around to it yet because it is not a priority" attitude speaks volume, and even if your heart is breaking to shreds right now, don't give him the satisfaction of knowing that.

Of course you don't need to be his 'Friend' to be able to see the stuff in his account on either Facebook or Twitter. You don't have to be an expert on social media to know that if he didn't secure his account with some heavy privacy settings, you will still be able to view it. So how do you survive that?

CHAPTER 11

HOW TO EMOTIONALLY SURVIVE LOOKING HIM UP ON THE INTERNET

When you log into your social media accounts, type his name and see he's posted a new photo of himself, you experience a head rush, dizziness and heart palpitations all at once. Of course you still love him, still want to be with him and somehow, since you are no longer with him, he appears to be even more handsome than before, hence the symptoms. However, you need to get yourself together right now and process this: he does not look any different than before and he definitely doesn't look any better! He couldn't have physically changed that much in a space of just a few days or weeks, so quit thinking he is a brand new man. I know your heart is breaking just by looking at him, but since you feel the compulsion to look him up, at least be realistic about what you are seeing and don't torture yourself with thoughts that are simply untrue. When I split up with my ex I was in a terrible position, because not only did my ex live his *entire* life on social networking sites, but in an attempt to get more publicity for his work, he also posted every tiny thing he ever worked on, on the internet! And as sad as it sounds, his work was his entire life, so I was able to view it unfolding day by day, minute after minute! You can imagine how, even when we were no longer connected by Facebook, I would visit his work website to see what he was doing, and what he currently looked like. On a bad day it would take as little as a new photo of him to upset me, and so I understand that even the most innocent of entries on a social media account can be extremely painful to view. That's why you need to read the next part very carefully.

CHAPTER 12

WHAT YOU ABSOLUTELY NEED TO KNOW BEFORE YOU SPY ON HIM ON FACEBOOK AND TWITTER

When you are looking at social media entries, including photos, you might get the impression that he's just carrying on like nothing happened, while you are devastated and are trying to get yourself together after the break-up. However, what you need to know is that *he is still very, very likely to be thinking about you and reminiscing about what you two had, no matter where he is, who he is with and how much he seems to be enjoying himself.* Because you are maintaining no contact, he won't know what is happening with you, and that thought alone is enough to make him wonder about you, at the very least.

If you were the one who finished the relationship with him due to his undesirable behavior (although you still wanted him and loved him deeply), consider this: when you see his newly added photos engaging with other people, whether it is on a night out with work mates, or on holiday with friends, *he may be putting on a bit of a show and he may not actually be enjoying himself as much as it seems because like you, he is heartbroken from the split.* Understand that, like you, he has good friends and they want to help him forget about you – but that doesn't actually mean that he can, or is, able to do so easily.

Don't presume that he is happy just because you see him smiling on his newly added Facebook or Twitter photos! He may appear to be without any worries, but if he was the one who dumped you and you are at the early stages of the break-up, remember, *he doesn't know what's coming to him!* He will soon realize that you are not groveling, not begging him for another chance, and that he was not irreplaceable. His smugness will not last very long. By the time he notices that you are not running around trying to get him back, he will most likely be looking for a way back to you. Concentrate on this and in the meantime wish him 'Happy Rejection'!

Understand that on social networking sites, people only put up photos that they have carefully chosen. If we were then compare it to a TV show, it would be a heavily edited one. So if you think in one of his newly added photos he looks smarter or happier than when he was with you, perhaps this is a deliberate image he is trying to create and maybe, just maybe – as he suspects you might be seeing it – *it is for your benefit!*

When you discover that he has been awarded a work promotion or had any other significant change in his life, *don't be upset or angry you have missed out and are not part of his life anymore*. You may even be partially responsible for his new achievement, because you were perhaps the one who drilled into his head that he could do better – that his previous job wasn't stimulating him enough, or that he is way smarter than he gave himself credit for. So now that you are currently not part of his life, know that he will remember that he was encouraged by you, and probably wishes you were there with him at the start of this new venture.

If you find out that he is doing something that during your relationship you two were planning to do together, consider that it will not come without a price for him, he will have to do it without you. A few weeks after my ex and I split up, I found out that he travelled to the Mediterranean coast, somewhere where I used to live, and still go back to very often. Although his travel was business not pleasure related, I took it badly, because it reminded me about the plans we were making of going there together. But when I got to properly thinking about it, I realized that he must have felt more upset than me. While I was at home getting on with my life, he was out there, being constantly reminded of me. He must have had me on his mind non-stop, so come to think of it and despite all his 'happy as Larry' photos in the sea, I knew he wasn't that happy to be there after all.

If you find out online that he has moved home, never, ever panic and start stalking him, either on the internet or in real life. If you happen to find out his new address, don't drive pass his house to see if he is in or if he is alone. Never question his friends about it either. The last thing he needs to know is that you care about his whereabouts. Yes, he is no longer at his old address, somewhere where you two had perhaps spent lovely days and nights, but consider this: because you are maintaining no contact with him, you are not going to go to his house anyway, so why would you need to know where he currently lives? It is a false sense of security that you always need to know where to find him, but remember, until he is ready to find you again, he doesn't want to be found! Concentrate on the fact that you are doing well and focus on the strength you are finding within yourself to deal with what's happened.

After you end your internet spying session, wipe away the tears, put some music on and put your feet up. I want you to consider that regardless of what you have just seen and read, and regardless of whatever has been said and done in your relationship, you still hold the power to change the situation to your advantage! It just takes time. I said it before and I will say it again; patience is a true virtue! Appreciate how strong you have been so far and consider that your new, composed behavior comes as a shock to your ex, who may have found you too much to deal with in the past. And remember this: if he is realizing that he has considerably misjudged you, it provides the first step for him to want to overturn the break-up. So be strong, and keep up the good work, no matter what you see on that computer screen! All that glitters is not gold!

CHAPTER 13

WHEN DEALING WITH HIS INTERNET LIFE BECOMES TOO MUCH TOO HANDLE

I am going to tell you a story of a girl I knew very well. This girl was going through a painful break-up, and soon after she stopped contact with her ex, she found herself on the internet finding out details about him. One day, as she holidayed abroad, she spotted on Facebook that her ex was also abroad, in fact very near to where she was staying. Within minutes she was looking at his holiday pictures and obsessing about the fact that he was having a good time without her (how very dare he?!). She was so preoccupied with him throughout her own holiday, that she spent all her time on the internet, reading his status updates, and viewing the photos of him frolicking in the sea. Prior to her departure she didn't even enjoy the last dinner with her friends, who frankly were very upset with her inability to let go and have fun with them. But the thought of him being carefree and happy, when she was still so unhappy, was all she could think of, and she ruined what was supposed to be a happy time away and a chance to get over him. Finally, as she was about to fly home the next day, she didn't check her flight was departing on schedule. The very next morning, and after a 50-minute drive to the airport, she entered the terminal building only to realize that her flight home had been cancelled. Of course there weren't many people at the airport, because everyone else had read the email from the airline the day before to say the flight was going to be grounded. She then had to admit to herself in embarrassment that she would have spared herself the expensive and long journey to the airport, and the wasted time, if she had just spent a single moment reading her emails instead of being glued to the pictures of her ex on his Facebook account.

I know how silly and angry she felt, because that girl was me, and that was the day I understood that I couldn't continue to be masochistic and prioritize him over me anymore. I never typed his name on my keypad again! Just like that, I reached closure on internet spying. And from that day on I knew that if I went there again I would allow him to dictate how I would feel and act, so I stopped for good. I'm not saying it wasn't tempting, but the idea of him having one over me, even after we were no longer together, made me sick to my stomach. There was no point in finding out what he had been up to or who with, we were over, and there was no need for me to know anything further about his life. Furthermore I decided not to give him the power to upset me anymore. And if looking him up meant getting myself in a state, I had to stop immediately. Don't give your ex the power to control your mood or behavior! By giving him such power you are also allowing him to affect your treatment of others; if you are in a bad mood it rubs off on other people, your priorities; you suddenly distract yourself from what is important and focus on him again, your productivity; you immediately lack motivation to do what you have initially set out to do and plunge into a hole of sadness – which leaves you powerless to do anything! When you've visited his account a few times and recognized it gets you down, STOP! Make a conscious decision and *stick to it*. You can triumph over the compulsion by remembering why you are no longer with him. Did he treat you well, with respect and like a lady? How did you part company? Did he ever promise and not deliver when it came to anything important? Remind yourself of his negative traits. Act with pride and aim higher than wasting your time thinking about someone who clearly doesn't deserve it.

CHAPTER 14

6-12 WEEKS AFTER THE BREAK-UP

Great news! You have managed to survive up to three months without any form of contact with your ex. In the last few weeks you've managed to put the pieces of your previously shattered existence back together, and you are not crying every time you hear a sad song on the radio or in the situations that bring back memories of him. Yes, understandably you are still sad but by now, you have accepted that the break-up took place, and you are no longer in a relationship with him. He does not preoccupy your mind in the same way as before, but having said that, you may still think about him several times a day. But it already feels different. The more causal your thoughts about him become, the more relaxed and composed you feel

Bizarrely, it is at this stage of the new routine of emotional balance in your life, that many women decide to break the no contact rule. This is perhaps because they think that since the detachment stage has been achieved, it might be okay to contact him now. Quite a lot of us believe that closure is needed to completely move on from an ex partner, and since there has been a considerable time, distance, silence and no contact between the two people involved, it will be easier to communicate. Let me tell you clearly that deciding to contact him now *would be the worst possible decision you could make!* Getting back in touch with your ex just weeks after a painful break-up is a terrible idea, and will only reignite the break-up pain. Beware of doing this. It could almost certainly reactivate the pain, and prove to him that you can't live without him even though you have tried.

If you have maintained no contact, 6-12 weeks after that break-up, your ex will be wondering why you are not making an effort to call him. He may also be thinking that you are just being stubborn, you are trying to play games, you have given up on him or that you no longer have feelings for him. Perhaps when you two were an item, he never bothered to fix the atmosphere after any argument you had. Perhaps you always took charge, responsibly and maturely approaching the conflict and always contacting him first to make up. And perhaps he just got lazy, because he got used to you doing all the work, which is a very bad habit to get into. Sure thing is, now he'll be wondering what's wrong. As I said before, you must make sure you allow him that special 'rejection', 'wallow in self-pity time', during which you grow stronger and heal. Remember, staying strong and not contacting him is not only about showing him that you don't need him, it's primarily about you not going back to old scenarios. It gives you the opportunity to break with the past and open a new chapter, or chapters, in your life. And this is the opportunity *you must* give yourself. You still feel the internal struggle, the head-against-heart battle, but you will be closer every day to winning that battle. I will mention one more time that to maintain up to 12 weeks of no contact with the person who used to fill your life not so long ago, is to be doing fantastically well. I want you to maintain that great work and motivate you to remain in your 'warrior mode'.

CHAPTER 15

WHAT EXACTLY IS 'WARRIOR MODE'?

When it comes to relationships, smart women must learn to exercise the power of the mind, in the same way sportsmen and women must to remain focused and win trophies and medals. But if you can bridge the gap between emotions and logic, you can be sure that you are a winner in the game of dating, relationships and break-ups. The idea is that you do not let any man drive you to lose control of your emotions. This is the difference between the winner's and the loser's attitude. The idea is to work on an emotional state and find that balance between emotion and logic – that's how you come to the tipping point which is 'warrior mode' – you may or may not have heard this expression. It's all to do with emotional control.

I urge you to work on your warrior mode, and if you know that you have gone too far in the emotional direction, pull yourself back to reach the right balance. While this might not be something you are very well trained in yet, you can treat the no contact rule as the right start to exercising the warrior mode. Emotional control is key. When you feel that you are reminiscing about your ex and are missing him to the point that you almost break your no contact rule, get yourself in your warrior mode. When you reach the stage of being in danger of allowing him to have one over you by emotionally dragging you down, fight your urges immediately making a list of negative and positive things associated with him. Here's an example of such list:

Positives: handsome; emotional; at times attentive to my needs; helpful with DIY; good listener when not busy; open minded and forward thinking

Negatives: stubborn; immature; never showed any initiative when it came to me; work always took priority; unable to see other's points of view; never accepted responsibility for anything; too easily influenced by what others, especially his friends, have to say; a 'one-minute man' in bed.

Did you notice how the list of negatives vastly outweighs the list of positives? Well, if it was the other way around, you two would still be an item, wouldn't you? But somehow, around the three-month mark, we choose to forget some of the more infuriating things in our exes behavior – things that led to the break-up. If you were to call him and tell him that you miss him, can't live without him and want him back, do you think he will miraculously become the opposite of these things you just listed under 'negatives'? There is unfortunately little chance of that happening. If he is ever to reappear in your life, he needs to make it on his own accord. He has to go through the process of almost being in 'no man's land' for a while, so he can process what has happened, this is the only way he will find out if he wants you back.

By remaining silent you are giving him the opportunity to realize two of the most important things in going forward:

That if he wants you back this will only happen if you become unavailable to him – giving him an opportunity to miss you and pursue you, or:

That although you and he may not be compatible enough to have another go at the relationship, you were far more of a classy act than he gave you credit for.

During this time you have to consider that in order to deal with your own emotions, you might want to avoid certain situations and people. So don't appear at a party where you know for a fact he will show up, just to see him and 'dazzle him', because chances are he will be less than pleased, and you could end up making a fool of yourself. Not to mention you could be left gutted and heartbroken if he shows a lack of interest in you.

Subsequently, don't accept any invitations from

friends of his; always politely decline. Intelligent people will know why you are doing this and will understand.

Don't appear at his workplace either, claiming that you want to use their services, because whatever it is that he does or produces, I'm sure that you can find that elsewhere. Don't fool yourself that he will see that as accidental, and remember that stalking is illegal!

When you slip up, and I mean slip up, when it comes to anything mentioned in this book, don't use it as an excuse to break down. In fact, don't you dare break down! Knowledge is power and you already have it! So just recap on what we have been saying, and if you need to, start reading previous chapters again to get back the motivation to survive.

This is now the time to start having realistic expectations and goals about your future. You no longer live in the past and to reinforce that, you must start new things in your life. Learning a new skill is a fantastic addition to your existing ones, but don't forget about what you already know.

These days the internet gives us incredible powers of self-promoting and publishing. When I engaged in my case studies about men who drive women crazy with their placid, unemotional behavior, I never expected to self-publish my findings into a book, but it happened! I have since realized how many people self-publish books, and that internet bookstores like Amazon or IBooks are booming. You only have to type whatever it is that interests you into Google, and there is a guarantee that one of the top searches will reveal a book on the subject.

So why not capitalize on the knowledge you already have? Are you an expert in dog grooming, backpacking on tighter than tight budgets or lactose-free cooking, and want to share your knowledge with the world? Why wait? Now is the perfect time to change your lonely evenings on the sofa into cooking seminars, for example. Cook, write recipes, take pictures, create a blog. And when it's ready, do some research on self-publishing and make it happen. It's easy and doesn't cost anything. And don't forget to share your book with me and my Twitter followers! Each and every one of us should identify areas of our expertise and give it a go in any way, shape or form to kill lonely, unfulfilled time and replace it with some fruitful and positive action. The possibilities are endless.

When you keep busy, you think less about your ex and create new environment that don't involve him. In other words, you are creating a brand new 'ex-free' zone. This is how you start moving on to other areas of life and slowly wipe him out of your existence. This is why it is so important to create new experiences, this helps to maintain motivation and continue with a strong will; which is vital to survival.

CHAPTER 16

3-6 MONTHS AFTER THE BREAK-UP

If you are reading this book just after your break-up, and have got to this stage, you may feel terrified that it will take this long to forget your ex. But I am going to tell you that there is no time limit on getting over a broken heart. It may take you a few weeks to completely stop thinking about him and realize that he was a loser, but it may take someone else six months, or more. Nothing is certain. It is as simple as that! The best you can do is to plough through with your head held high.

There is good news, girlfriend, the worst appears to be behind you! Polish up your sharp wisdom every day, stick by your newly created set of rules, and keep improving your knowledge.

Time to get rid of his stuff

When I said before that you should keep some of his belongings, text messages and emails, I warned that the time will come when you need to get rid of them. Well, the time is now! Now you have survived the initial shock of the break-up and the overwhelming pain of the last few weeks, you are ready to part with the past that represents him. Under no circumstances though, you should use this as an excuse to contact him to return his belongings. Let's just presume that since he was doing fine without them until now, he doesn't need them anymore. Throw them straight where they belong; in the waste bin, or burn them in the bucket in your backyard. Remember to do this safely!

His emails to you, his text messages and other forms of written communications like letters or posted notes, should share the fate of his belongings. If you feel you are still not ready to let go, I will insist that you trust me on this and get rid of this stuff anyway. There is a reason you must do this; you can't keep living in the past! I know it hurts and I know it is hard to let go. Like you, I was there, but this is crucial if you want to progress and forget about him. Even if you are initially not convinced, you will feel better after doing it.

Empower yourself

Could this break-up mean re-birth for you? If you are still struggling with letting go of him emotionally, or his belongings, empower yourself with a little parting ceremony. Invite friends for some drinks and get rid of his stuff that night. It's a good idea to be supported by friends when you do this. There is a possibility that this will be upsetting, but it will not last long however, and it may be purifying.

At home you can light a candle and burn his photos, etc, in the flame, if you feel you need to. But please do this very carefully! Imagine the light as a new powerful force that now glows inside you and portray it as new energy to keep you going. Whenever you feel down refer to this energy as a source of comfort with positive healing qualities. It now shines inside you and you own it.

Re-train your brain by repeating positive thoughts and statements

Remember positive statements? Keep producing them and read them to yourself every morning and every night. Remember they have to be as strong, or stronger, than the negative statements that cloud your mind. Write a powerful prayer and read it every day with your positive statements. *Believe* in your success, *believe* that you can and will get over him for good and very soon. Use this experience to change your outlook on life and men in the process. As discussed before, don't make the same mistakes again! It will benefit your entire future.

Here are some examples of positive statements:

"I am strong and will get over him."

"He did not deserve me."

"I deserve a man who pursues me, fights for me and cares for me."

"I am not going to put any more energy into thinking about or pursuing my ex."

"Life is about opportunity, and from now on I will take every single one that comes my way."

"I will not give up after setbacks."

"I will make myself a success."

"I am better off without him because I am now stress-free and have more time for myself and my friends."

"Everything happens for a reason and this break-up was no different."

Surround yourself with true friends and get rid of anyone who drains you

Starting a new chapter in life is a momentous occasion and deserves to be followed by changes in other areas of your life. Now that you literally live by the rule 'good riddance to bad rubbish', apply it elsewhere. If you feel that there are people in your life who drain you, cut contact with them. Don't feel guilty, it takes guts to do that and you have your reasons. *Your* well-being is priority! Subsequently if you feel that some people are trying to sabotage your good work, get rid of them as well. There are people who pretend to be friends, act as friends, and perhaps believe that they are your friends – but they give you conflicting advice and create confusion in your head. Any friend who tells you that you are to pursue and fight for him is wrong and don't allow them to ruin your good work.

You are responsible for your own happiness; don't let anyone abuse you

If you feel that someone is taking advantage of your good nature, stop them! Don't rely on anyone to make you happy or complete. It is your job to do that for yourself. Don't let any other man use you, and don't ever volunteer to do for any new man in your life what he has not done for you first. Don't give him too much of your time and attention until he proves he is worth it. Evaluate what love is. Is love the quick "I love you" spoken quickly at the end of the conversation on the phone? Or is it looking after you and standing by you when you are ill, unwell, depressed or confused? Prepare a list of things you are looking for in a man and read it at least once a week. Never, EVER continue seeing a man who from the very beginning of the relationship has been sending mixed messages like:

"I'll do anything for you/I can't see you."

"I've never felt about any woman the way I feel about you/I think some space will do us both good."

"Of course I want us to move in together/I need my own creative space or I'm grumpy."

That kind of a man is called an emotional wimp, and for variety of reasons he will slowly but surely start to make you feel rejected, abandoned, devalued, not good enough and low about yourself no matter how confident you naturally are. This will only lead to frustration, anger, devastation, humiliation, insecurity and depression. It is essential for your well-being that you recognize the signs early and run for the hills.

Visualize don't fantasize

It is very important to recognize that a break-up can sometimes make us women pursue an imaginary relationship with our ex. Women who have been hurt, sometimes idealize their exes and fantasize about them. It is a way of defying what has happened and remaining in a fantasy world – also known as denial. I guess you can easily detect what I am going to say next: this is not a good idea! To let go of your ex, you must keep in mind at all times why you two have split up. That's why it is good to turn to your list of his negative traits, to keep reinforcing that he was in fact no saint, to say the least. The fact that he took you on holiday once does not actually mean that he was full of initiative. In the same way - introducing you to his parents doesn't mean he wanted life-time commitment. Attributing him with non- existent positives will only cause confusion in your head, so think straight and don't allow yourself to be lead astray by your imagination.

This is very different to always trying to see the good in a person, of course we must do that, but we have to be realistic here – remembering the reasons why you split, and the parts of his personality that constantly hurt or angered you, will help you to put him and the break-up into perspective.

Accept your reality

When you accept 'what is', you are truly clearing your path to true happiness; you will remove all obstacles standing in your way. There is no easy way to get there, or a short cut to get there more quickly. You need to go through all stages of it at your own individual pace to get to acceptance.

It is also important to find out if your ex is making you re-live the drama from past relationships, or even your childhood, by pushing buttons that have been pushed way before he appeared in your life. You may not even be aware of it, but this can be a reason you are struggling to let go completely. If so, seek out a trained therapist, because getting rid of a negative blockage of emotions might be the only way of understanding your behavior, which in turn might be the only way of moving on.

If you feel you need closure from your ex in order to get rid of anger and resentment towards him, think again. For many people coping with break-ups all over the world, closure is a non-existent thing. The only people who achieve it are the people who plan to break up with their partners, and know in advance that's what they are going to do. Forget about closure and instead recognize that sometimes you just have to accept how life pans out. Follow your new life path and never look back.

PART 3

IMPORTANT QUESTIONS AND ANSWERS ABOUT YOUR BREAK-UP

CHAPTER 17

WHEN WILL HE REALIZE YOU HAVE STOPPED THE CONTACT FOR GOOD AND WHAT IT DOES TO HIM?

There are few questions you need to ask yourself in order to answer the above. Have you two ever broken up before? Perhaps you have let your emotions get the better of you and called him after, let's say three weeks? Let's just presume that was the case. He may deliberately avoid thinking about your absence from his life for the first few weeks, but eventually he will have to analyze what happened, even if it was he who wanted to break up, to be single, free and date other women. Trust me on this, you may think that men like him do not place any importance on dates, times, anniversaries, etc, but believe me they do, and never more so when it is something as important as the day you two last spoke, and after he just realized that you may be gone for good. After all, he has a morbidly obese ego and this ego is not used to dieting. When the time you usually would have got in touch is up, he will be going through his phone, and he will know exactly that the last message from you came on Tuesday at 11.23am, and the last time he heard your voice was 20 minutes later. *He knows* - be sure of that. He will be going through that phone every lonely evening re-reading those last messages, because he is just starting to realize he messed it all up, and he may never receive a message from you again.

You may be dying to speak to him or want find out what he did after the break-up. I know you are going through an internal struggle. But just know that he has no idea that you are struggling so much. For all you know he thinks you are single again and having a great time, perhaps even engaging with other men, and the thought of that is probably driving him crazy. He must be thinking that, because he knows how attentive and mad about him you were, and how you always went back for more. So he will be assuming that you have transferred these feelings onto someone better than him, or that you finally understand that he wasn't that special after all, and you are enjoying being single and happy.

CHAPTER 18

IF I WANT HIM BACK, SHOULD I BE SEEN WITH OTHER MEN TO MAKE HIM JEALOUS?

The answer here is simple - ABSOLUTELY NOT! This is not to avoid breaking his precious heart, or to spare him feelings of distress, far from it. But rather, if you want him to feel deep regret that you two are no longer an item, you must first and foremost behave like a class act. And throwing yourself into the arms of an army of different men, or even just one man, will only confirm to him that he was right to let you go. It is not the right thing to do to try to prove to him that you did not care and can easily replace him.

Your job is to show him that even though your heart is breaking because you loved him, you can handle your emotions; you have enough pride and dignity to walk away and endure the pain with your head held high.

Your job is to show him he pulled the plug on the unlimited amount of love that he would have had from you, and that he was wanted and needed.

Your job is to make him realize that you valued yourself enough to walk away – even if it took a long time for you to get to that point. Eventually he will realize that you are very special in his eyes.

Imagine if he actually wanted to get back together with you and found out you were seen on the arm of someone else? And even if he doesn't want to get back together, as I mentioned before, you can't make him think he was easily replaceable, because that simply isn't true. If it were true, you wouldn't be reading this book. Besides, the last thing you want is for the truth to actually come out, and that is that you were only doing it to make him jealous; that would make you look pathetic. You already hold the power because you've stopped contacting him, and now you must make sure you keep up the good work!

CHAPTER 19

WHAT IF WITHIN THIS TIME I WILL MEET SOMEONE I REALLY LIKE?

There are no rules and regulations when it comes to how and when Mr. Right will come into your life. However there are such things as choices.

I am sure you are probably aware that the last thing I want to pass on to women through this book, is that since they got dumped, or were forced to dump their partners, they must live their lives like nuns and never experience happiness again. But just think - how soon will you really be ready for a new relationship? If you are the kind of woman who has never spent any considerable time being single, perhaps now is the right time to figure out stuff about yourself, and to remain on your own for a while? I bet you never thought you could gain much understanding of your behavior through remaining single, but the fact is, being single is the *best time* to truly learn to understand ourselves and our capacity to love other human beings.

Our true knowledge of what we are capable of, and how we love, does not actually come from our experiences with men. It comes to us when we are concentrating on *ourselves* and learning about *ourselves*. If you allow yourself that precious time on your own, you will understand that being single doesn't actually mean being lonely, and you will perhaps learn to walk away from a relationship which is not making you happy much earlier that you actually have before.

One of the reasons we remain in unhappy, unfulfilling relationships is fear. This is the fear of not finding another partner who is as great as the current one. But of course, since the current (or perhaps now the ex partner) isn't actually that great, it is just the fear of loneliness you are experiencing. Remaining single for few months doesn't mean you will never find a man again, in fact it is quite the opposite. Undamaged men are (mostly) attracted to single and available women, and they welcome the information that you have not had a man in your life for few months. That way they can be sure that the competition (your ex) is out of the picture, and you are not on the rebound.

Having said all that, I bet that somewhere out there, there are women who have walked out of the arms of Mr. Wrong straight into the arms of Mr. Right! How did that happen, you may ask? And I will tell you how - if this new relationship became something substantial and serious, it was because these women did not rush them, and because it wasn't about replacing their ex with a new man. So the moral of the story is this: if you meet a great guy shortly after the break-up, make sure you do not become the sad statistic of 'too much too soon'. Instead, let this man know that you have just separated from your ex and are still recovering from the break-up, but would very much appreciate a light-hearted friendship and just see what happens in the future.

CHAPTER 20

CAN I HAVE A 'FRIENDS WITH BENEFITS' RELATIONSHIP WITH ANOTHER MAN IF I WANT MY EX BACK, AND WHILE I'M WAITING ON HIM TO CALL?

Many women believe that since their last partner would not commit to them, it was somehow their fault and they feel unworthy of another committed relationship. For all these women, who frankly, could not be more wrong, I recommend reading my book *It Really Is All His Fault* to get some much needed perspective on the issue. Truth is, sometimes after enduring the pain of an unfulfilled relationship, we decide to take the 'friends with benefits' route because we no longer want to deal with complicated emotions. But is this the right way forward directly after a break-up?

Not all women feel the need to have committed relationships. But even the women who make conscience decisions to remain in casual relationships have no guarantee that these will not end up becoming serious - which will involve dealing with emotions. You may have had many casual relationships with men in your life, and you never knew that the next would become the love of your life, or, the man who after you gave him your heart decided to smash it. There is never a good moment in life to deal with that, but I can tell you that there is definitely a worse one: when you are still licking your wounds from the experiences of your previous relationship. If the new casual fling goes wrong and leaves you brokenhearted, it may even make you want to contact your ex, perhaps in order to seek reassurance or credibility. And just imagine how bad you would feel if he ignored your call or never got back. Suddenly you would be dealing with not only your latest heartbreak, but also with your ex, the rejection they *both* made you feel and a massively harmed self-esteem. Besides, giving men the 'no strings attached' line, means you will never be able to expect anything more serious.

Life is not a movie starring Justin Timberlake (*Friends with Benefits*). Men who enter into these arrangements with intelligent and attractive women, cannot believe how lucky they are, but at least they are honest from the beginning. They are not looking for love and you must never kid yourself that they are. Men in these situations don't wake up one day and decide to make such relationships serious. Truth is, they are probably grieving from their previous relationship not working out, or buying some time before they decide to call their own exes. Some are just narcissistic, and the rest are commitment phobes. There is nothing more to it!

When your pride and self-esteem has just suffered massively, you quickly want to re-build it with some much needed attention from the opposite sex. It is your life and only you know how to live it, but I strongly advise you to leave 'friends with benefits' on your DVD shelf.

CHAPTER 21

SHOULD I STAY FRIENDS WITH MY EX AFTER THE BREAK-UP?

This is, in fact a big, big no, no! Making your ex regret the break-up is to make him realize that he has lost you, otherwise he will never realize how your absence has affected him, so you can't hover on sideline pretending to be his friend. If he asked you to be his friend when he was breaking up with you, make sure you take his words for what they actually are, a pile of "I pity you" rubbish. You don't want him to feel sorry for you. Besides, he is actually only asking you to be his friend because he wants to ease his conscience because he just dumped you, that's all. You don't want to be making anything that easy for him.

You have to read between the lines, because at this stage he doesn't actually know what he is saying, or does not mean it like you think he does. If you remain in his life you will always be available for him to call you and see you, so you might as well stick a 'doormat' note on your forehead. Because this is what will actually make him realize he has it all: a new single life to date other women and you at his beck and call when he has no other plans. I bet he wouldn't have any problem convincing you that occasional break-up sex is not a bad idea either, if he runs out of other options. If I'm still not managing to convince you that this is a bad idea, just think how upset you would be if during one of these friendly encounters with him, he reveals that he is dating someone else, or that his new relationship is serious, or started telling you about the trouble in his new relationship! Yes, you might think that this is a bit extreme, but trust me, I would not put it past some men! I'll tell you exactly how you would feel: devastated; angry; humiliated; de-valued; not good enough and yes, you would be asking yourself that difficult question too if he tells you his latest relationship is serious: "Why not me?"

You have the emotional and mental capacity to remain at a distance from him, and this distance tells him that you are not as desperate as he thought you were to keep him in your life and to accept just any role in it because… he is like a Chanel bag actually.

One of my close friends, whose name is Brittany, was recently dumped by her ex. Of course she was hurt and furious, but she got one over him when he asked her to remain friends with him, to which she said: "No thanks, you are like a Chanel bag, I wanted you but I don't desperately need you and I have friends already, thank you very much." I thought this was brilliant because within these two short sentences she had managed to let him know that she was never, and certainly not now, ever that desperate for him. She also made quite clear that she wasn't going to settle for just anything for the pleasure of remaining in his life, and managed to make him question just how much she'd actually loved him, which was enough for him to feel rejected.

Not remaining friends with your ex sends a powerful message: I DON'T NEED YOU! You decided to exclude me from your life and so you have to accept the consequences; you will not see or hear from me anymore. If he left you with no choice but to break up with him, you're clearly letting him know: your behaviour was so overwhelmingly painful to endure that I would rather not have you in my life at all, than accept what you were prepared to give me, which was not very much and certainly not good enough. That would make any man feel incredibly anxious, because when it comes to matters of the heart, decision making and sticking to it, it is not as straight forward as you would expect. It would almost immediately make him question his decision to part ways with you!

When you show him that you respect yourself and can't be played, he knows that you mean business. If a man tells you that he would like to remain friends after he has just told you that he no longer wants a relationship with you, you do have the option to tell him that you hope to remain friends to avoid extra drama, but *never contact him again*. If he calls, don't pick up the phone. Don't reply to his texts or emails, simply continue ignoring him. At the beginning, blissfully unaware, he will think that he is still at liberty to contact you whenever he feels like it, but after few unfruitful attempts to speak to you, he will realize that this is not the case. When you show strength, emotional restraint and an unwillingness to please him, he will feel abandonment. Smart women know that nothing is as cool and rewarding as reversing a situation that looked hopeless for her, but has instead managed to turn everything around to her advantage. And even if nothing will ever happen between the two of you again, you will always be that girl who kept her cool and resisted the temptation of seeing him again. Of course question is: will he be able to do the same?

CHAPTER 22

IF WE ARE MEANT TO BE TOGETHER AND I AM CURRENTLY NOT CONTACTING HIM, HOW LONG WILL IT TAKE FOR HIM TO CALL ME?

This is unfortunately not as simple as adding two and two together and making it four. Why? Because every human being has their own personality, life experience, character and free will. Therefore if your friend has previously applied the no contact rule and heard from her ex after three weeks, but you are still waiting, having done exactly the same, you must not get impatient, call him and undo all your hard work. By doing this you will lose all credibility, and it still doesn't mean that he wasn't going to call.

Once, when my ex and I had a serious argument, I stopped contacting him. Previously I would always call to reverse the damage, but not this time. I had not spoken to him for over two weeks. I was angry and I didn't actually want to hear from him. Nevertheless he texted me out of the blue one evening when he was out of the country, saying that he missed me and that he hoped I was okay. It wasn't much, but I knew that for him it was a huge step, and I knew how much he actually must have be missing me to press that 'Send' button.

If your relationship is meant to be your ex will eventually call you. When? Some men will be more mature than others, or more willing to admit to their mistakes, which will speed up the process of getting back in contact and getting back together. But others might be immature and childish. They may have been brought up in an environment where they had to have their way and they have continued to behave that way throughout their adult life. These men are very difficult to deal with, having said that, it is not impossible to deal with them, because even the most selfish of men have feelings, they just have to be allowed the time to realize these feelings.

Some men are so stubborn that they will think nothing of hurting themselves, just for the sake of not gratifying you. And some are simply in denial and overestimate their own abilities to keep women hanging on. It might be of some consolation to you if I tell you that these men are the most likely to be thinking about you non- stop. They will be waking up with you on their mind every morning, thinking about you during the day and you will be the very last thing on their mind before they go to sleep. And as time passes they will move through different stages of their new single life and with each day they will be making the discovery that the grass is not greener, which will eventually force them to consider if their stubbornness is worth the loneliness.

CHAPTER 23

WHAT YOU GAINED BY SEPARATING FROM HIM

When relationships go really wrong, sooner or later they will end. As much as the split from a man you love is one of the most painful things to endure, I hope, that by now you understand that distance and silence is needed in order to reflect on the relationship, and where things were simply not working out.

When you reflect back on the time you were with him, you realize the amount of effort and time you put into making that relationship work. This could have actually been time used or invested into something that could have benefited your career or your bank account balance. However, I know that more than anything else in the world, us women want to be in committed relationships that make us feel loved and secure, that's why you probably don't regret your time spent with him, and that's perfectly alright, because having regrets is a big waste of anyone's time. However, only fools refuse to learn from bad, painful experiences, so be sure to draw your own conclusions about where you have possibly gone wrong.

The reality now is, you are no longer together, even if it is only temporarily. As much as we talked about various painful emotions, you must embrace the fact that the split from him has not only brought you pain, but power too. You have also learned liberation and can now enjoy some obvious advantages that have arisen from the situation.

Most important things you have gained by freeing yourself from him:

Time - Yes, you might think: "I don't want time on my own, I'd much rather be with him". But trust me, when you reflect back on this period, you will be counting it as a blessing. This is quite literally the best time for you to get to know yourself better. Never spent any or little time on your own before? Now is the perfect opportunity to do so! When you learn how fun time spent with yourself can be, and as you slowly start to incorporate various things into your newly single life, (including men), don't make the mistake of sacrificing your 'me time' again. This time is precious, and should stay that way.

Personal development opportunities - When the emotions can be controlled more easily and the initial shock of the situation has worn off, now is the right time to go out there and venture into other things, like learning new skills or becoming a member of a health club. You never know what the new activities you decide to take up will lead to, they may be beneficial for your career, or you may make great new friends. Think about it like this, when you were with your ex, you could not even think about taking a Spanish language course, for example, because you spent all your free time with him. Yet every year when you went on holiday, perhaps you were faced with the nightmare of almost non-existent communication with the locals, because you only understood few basic expressions. Impress your girlfriends and learn something that you cannot only showcase to the rest your friends, but will actually be beneficial for you. The opportunities are endless, you only have to give yourself a chance to do something, and want to put yourself out there.

An opportunity to meet Mr. Right - Yes, that's right and even if you currently don't feel ready to date, know that the path is wide open for a new man to, sooner or later, arrive in your life.

Money - When I was in the relationship with my ex, all I thought about was how to spend my money on things related to him, or doing stuff with him. On one occasion, as he was permanently broke, I even lent him money which he never bothered to return. Perhaps you have gone down that same route. If you can for a moment focus on how your expenditure looked while you were with him, you will no doubt realize that you spent a small fortune on things related to the relationship with him. These things included impulse or one-off purchases of clothing, or make-up products which you only bought to impress him, extra food you bought and cooked to feed him (and impress him) and travelling money you spent going to see him. For some women, this list would not be exclusive of paying for holidays, theatre or cinema tickets, days out, restaurant meals, short breaks away, etc. Start appreciating that no one is draining your bank account anymore, and you can make sensible purchases, as well as treating yourself to something special occasionally. It's untrue that money is unimportant - money matters - and now you have full control over how you spend yours, you'd better spend it on something that will make you and only you happy!

Understanding that life goes on - and that even the worse break-up pain will come to pass. You now have that knowledge, together with the advantage of understanding the break-up process and knowing how to get through it with your head held high. Who knows, maybe you can guide a friend through it next time, or use this experience to teach yourself that no man will put you in a state of such misery again. One thing is certain, you have regained your...

Independence + Self sufficiency = Self-esteem - Because you've been through a break-up process and accepted that you are now single, you understand that you are able to stand on your own two feet and you don't need a man in your life just for the sake of having one. If you have spent most of your adult life being in relationships - enjoy your independence: no need to make your plans around that other person; no need to consult anyone about anything; no need to compromise. Consider how self sufficient you have become and notice how much self-esteem you can draw from that!

A kick start to a healthy diet - Due to initial shock and the pain of the break-up, many of us lose weight. This may however, be the perfect opportunity to change your diet and embark on a healthier one. Perhaps you always wanted to lose weight but never really knew how to start the initial weight loss? If you have lost inches off your waist, you now know you can do it! So why not continue with the good work? You may find that it could just be one of many…

Blessings in disguise - When my ex and I broke up, I was devastated, like any other woman would be. But little did I know at the time that the experience he provided me with would be enough to write two books and start selling them in over 170 countries! You just don't know what the future will bring! One thing is certain: your break-up was just a path to other, better, more interesting, more beneficial things which you will discover with time and, trust me, you will be happy that you were given these new opportunities!

CHAPTER 24

WHAT HE LOST BY SEPARATING FROM YOU

Any guy who experiences no contact from a woman he dumped will eventually realize how deeply he misses her. Even the most stubborn of men experience regret that these (and other) perks of being someone's boyfriend no longer apply.

Self-esteem - A few weeks after the break-up, even the most confident of men will be drawn into the dark place called 'rejection'. After all, your lack of contact is not what he expected. Furthermore, he was probably considering changing his number so you won't bother him again and... oh, a little surprise, you don't seem to call him at all! Just look at where that got him. On a scale of zero to ten, how much good do you think that will do his over-blown ego? Zero? I'd say five.

Regular sex - This was one of the most pleasurable benefits he drew from a relationship with you, and now he has to live with the fact that it's not easily available. Yes, he might stumble upon a willing one-night-stand girl, get lucky with someone else, or even pay for it, but a good woman with great standards and visually pleasing is not something that is there on a plate anymore and easy to access without any effort.

Your support - When you were together, you supported every personal and professional move he made by being there for him and wishing him well. Maybe you even physically helped him when he needed you, and were happy to devote your time to improve his life or career? Well, that's all lost now too.

Attention & admiration - Make no mistake, men DO need both these things even more than women! The only difference is, they rarely ask their girlfriend to give them a cuddle or ask about how they look, what color suits them or if they are sexy. Regardless of the fact he never asked, you still told him repeatedly how smart, sexy, interesting and attractive he was, didn't you? Men are brought up to control and hide their true emotions, but they also occasionally need reassurance or a hug, because they are human. I can't see him going to his best mate to get that, can you?

Quality time spent with you - lack of which will eventually equal loneliness: sad evenings in front of the TV after work; no one to share that pizza with.

As they say, careful what you wish for...

The boyfriend status - Do you know that men amount to over 65 per cent of online daters? The latest survey on online relationships revealed that it is in fact men who are in the majority when it comes to wanting internet encounters. Consider that although the ratio of women to men in this world still technically gives men a privilege of wider choice, how much wider is it really? Getting a girlfriend who a man is compatible with and more importantly, shares his standards and meets his visual preferences, is not very easy at all. Right now, he is just another single guy looking to pull. And he already had it all... What a shame!

PART 4

GETTING BACK TOGETHER

CHAPTER 25

HOW TO REACT TO A TEXT OR EMAIL FROM HIM

It might have taken him days, weeks or even months but one day he gets in touch.

Perhaps you always wanted to get back together and used the no contact rule to make him realize certain things. Or maybe you have already let go of him, but the sudden contact has brought back memories. Do you think he might be worth another go? Before you euphorically reply to his text or email or decide to pick up that phone and have a conversation with him *take steps to ensure that you have control over the situation and don't give in to emotions.* Let me run through few points with you.

First things first, if you were waiting for him to make the first move to get back together, prepare yourself for the fact that his message may mean nothing else to him but to prove that he can still have you when he only chooses to. *It is very important to remain grounded and analyze the situation carefully.*

If he had texted or emailed you, in other words if he had chosen written word as the means of making contact, he has put himself in a slightly more comfortable position than calling, because by writing and waiting for reply he doesn't run the possibility of an instant rejection, which would happen if you chose not to answer the call. When he is waiting for you to reply, be sure that it is as nauseous and nerve-wracking for him as possible. Beware of becoming overly excited and typing back as if nothing else was more important. You need to leave it for a couple of weeks to reply and when you do get back, NEVER make excuses for your late answer. Why? Well, have you ever heard any respectable woman making excuses for lateness to a man?

What do you think about this: *"Hi, so sorry for the late message, I deleted your email address after you broke up with me and your last message went straight to my junk folder. I only just found it, so replying promptly!"* If you decide to send something along those lines, you might as well add: *"Replying promptly because I have no life, no friends, nothing to do and now that you have graced my mailbox again with your presence, I should probably stick that doormat note I kept in my drawer back on my forehead!"*

Are you getting my drift? Under no circumstances are you to take the role of the person who apologizes! Under no circumstances are you to start groveling!

The most important thing before you reply is to identify why he has got back in touch. Does he want something from you? Does his message suggest that he wants to be friendly (why would he want to be friends?). Or is he perhaps thinking about rekindling the relationship with you? Perhaps the wording of his message is making the nature of his interest in you unclear, because he only wants to test the waters to avoid possible embarrassment?

Here are some examples of various possible written messages:

"Hello. How are you? Was thinking about you recently and decided to see how you were. Write back, hope you're okay anyway x"

He is definitely testing the waters! It may not mean he only wants an instant upgrade of his ego, but you need to be careful. Be two steps ahead and always reply to such message in a way that, whatever happens next, your pride will be intact:

"Hello. I am very well and keeping quite busy. Hope you're okay."

Never engage in anything else because a 'testing the waters' does not deserve a different style of reply. Remember, be two steps ahead. Don't ask how he is, because that question would then open up communication, which in return would make it easy for him to reply with another 'no substance' message. However, it is good manners to say, "Hope you're okay".

Don't include anything like, "Nice to hear from you again", or "Hello stranger". These kind of sentences are reserved for friends who you have not heard from for some time, not for ex-boyfriends who misbehaved and are suddenly crawling out of the woodwork. A simple "Hello" will do. Let him know that you are well and are keeping busy, but don't go into details, because if you have time to elaborate, it means you are not that busy after all! Refrain from using sentences like: "I'm great, just fab really", it stinks of a lie and game playing. Never end a message with a kiss, even if he has puts ten at the end of his. If you keep the stance of serious business he will instantly get that. Then, expect a delay in his reply, because he now has to think long and hard about how to approach you again. In the meantime, if you really want to hear from him, don't go torturing yourself that you put him off because you have not been friendly enough, or demonstrated enough enthusiasm. If you want a man to pursue you and fight for your affections you will have to put him through the mill. If you make it easy for him (again) it's 'game over', you will never earn his respect. Unless you want to run circles around a man who will eventually dump you (again) for a more challenging woman, be smart, switch on your 'warrior mode' and don't allow yourself to get carried away.

If he texts or emails with anything like:

"Hello, how are you? Was thinking about you recently and decided to see how you were. I recently ran the charity marathon which I took you to watch with me last year and it brought back a lot of good memories. Anyway, write back if you fancy a chat x"

There is a lot more detail here. This is more of an emotional statement, which proves that you do come to his mind when he finds himself in situations he had previously shared with you. However, there is definitely no need to go overboard with your reply. Remember be two steps ahead.

"Hi, I'm very well, thank you. Good to hear you are keeping fit. I also remember it being a good day. Hope you're okay."

Notice how you are:

Firstly: NOT acting on what he has communicated in an emotional manner: "Good to hear you are keeping fit", although you are acknowledging what he had said. You are one step ahead.

Secondly: NOT asking how he is, but are not compromising your manners by adding: "Hope you're okay." You are two steps ahead!

Again, don't place anything but perhaps your name at the end of the message. No kisses and no pet names! If you want your ex back in your life you need to let him know from the very beginning that he is not dealing with the old, all-accepting and ever-forgiving you. The first lesson should be him patiently waiting for you to message back. Not replying to 'no substance' messages and not elaborating with 'sweet nothings' means he hasn't got an easy job of getting close to you again. So he immediately realizes that he needs to step up.

Maybe this is even the first time he will have the chance to pursue you. Maybe you did not give him that opportunity before? If he was counting on an easy ride, he will be disappointed, and you will spare yourself more heartache. If he is serious about getting close to you again, he will have to do the hard work. If you set your standards high from the very beginning, there will never be any confusion in his head as to how he needs to treat you. Reflect your expectations in your behavior, and allow him to figure out on his own if and how he wants to act upon it.

While you may be on cloud nine that he is back in touch with you, be aware of sudden impulses that would nudge you towards writing him an emotionally charged email or text. In fact don't show any emotions at all. Many women believe that to create closeness and intimacy they need to tell a man how painful, difficult and agonizing the break-up was for them and how they never stopped loving them. Let me ask you this: do you have to tell anybody that daffodils are yellow and roses are red? Well it's obvious isn't it? As obvious as the fact that you were suffering - but he doesn't need to know the details.

But let's get back to our text messages or emails. If he writes back:

"I have been very busy at work, even got promoted recently, but it somehow doesn't make me as happy as it should and I think one of the reasons for this is the fact we are no longer together x"

This is a brave statement to make. It tells you that he is missing you. However, it doesn't mean you are to drop your guard instantly either. Messages like this mean that he is not interested in playing games and is putting his cards on the table. It takes a mature man to decide to act that way, especially if he was the one who broke up with you, because it is also partially an admission that he made a mistake. You can engage in mature and un-emotional communication here. Don't bring up the past and don't dwell on the break-up pain. Instead, also accept responsibility for your part in the break-up. You don't have to go into details, you only need to say: "I recognized my mistakes and I have learnt from them."

But what are you to do if little interest is generated by your reply, (remember, 'no substance' messages deserve 'no substance' replies, and nothing else!), he has not gotten in touch again? Nothing! Absolutely nothing! In fact there is one thing you can do: count your blessings that you have not let that hopeless man back into your life to cause you pain and real havoc! Just think, if he was counting on an easy ride, he'll be very disappointed. And so he should be! If he wanted an instant boost to his self-esteem by proving to himself that getting you back was a doddle, he badly miscalculated that one, didn't he? More importantly, he finally understands that you are a classy act! Trust me, you don't need men like him around draining you and using you. You can do way better than him. He also now knows that's the case.

To conclude this section, when a man you loved or still love gets back in touch with you, he brings back old memories of the relationship you had with him. At this point I advise you to take his messages for what they are and not fantasize about him and idealize him. Always read his words carefully and use your mind not your emotions to reply. Don't expect anything! Considering the heart-break you have been through, ask yourself if the man who has put you through this is really worth another try, which you are effectively granting by replying to him. Consider how well you have done by separating from him. Let your wellbeing be the first priority, and ensure that you don't do yourself further damage by handling this badly. If you want him back, there will be plenty of time for emotions when you play your cards right and get back together with him.

CHAPTER 26

HOW TO HANDLE THE FIRST PHONE CALL FROM HIM

If some time after the break-up he gets in touch by calling, as much as you may want to pick up the phone, DON'T! Being too available did not get you far last time. Don't worry that he will not call again. If he truly cares for you and wants to re-establish contact with you, he will get in touch again. If he only called to 'test the waters' and you were unresponsive, he is unlikely to call again unless he is severely emotionally insecure and needs to prove to himself that he can conquer and achieve.

When you see your ex's number on your phone for the first time in weeks or months, your heart starts going so fast you may actually get dizzy. As much as your first instinct is to pick up and hear his voice, I urge you to remain unresponsive. If he leaves a message, listen to it and control your emotions. If it has been months since you two last spoke and you'd lost hope that you would ever hear from him again, you might actually experience slight shock. Therefore it is so important that you do not act or say anything on impulse. If he left a message, play it back and analyze it. If the message is casual and contains no real information, in other words it has no substance, don't reply. Here's an example of such message:

"Hey it's John. How're you doing? Give me a call sometime. Take care!"

The first thing you need to understand about such a message is that, as well as being everything I just mentioned, it is also borderline disrespectful. For a man, who when you last spoke to him, told you he doesn't want a relationship with you anymore, sending such message is pathetic and immature. It is a very 'safely played' message, composed that way for fear of not losing face if the woman was to avoid picking up the phone or getting back to him. It leaves him with variety of open options - he could even pretend that the message was intended for someone else. That's why under no circumstances should you be thinking of rewarding him with a reply, at least until he can come up with something a bit better, and if he wants you back, trust me, he will!

If a message from your ex contains material of more emotional nature, stay guarded. The fact the he has just reminded himself of your existence does not mean that you have to jump to attention. When you are ready and decide to call him back, be prepared that he may not pick up the phone instantly. Consider that before you make the phone call. If he doesn't call back within 24 hours, forget about him and don't respond to any other form of contact. If, within a week from your phone call, he calls you back and leaves some ridiculous message with a pathetic excuse, don't fall for it - unless he has been in some horrific car crash, for example, and you choose to visit him in hospital. The point is, you don't want to settle for scraps again, do you? And if he values contact with you, he will be back on that phone to you within a day.

Very rarely does a man who is serious about you call again on the same day if you haven't replied to him yet, which gives you plenty of time to compose your answer. If a message from him is in any way disrespectful or abusive, delete it and never reply. If you encourage unwanted and pointless contact by replying you are fueling his further actions. If it persists, change your number.

The more emotionally insecure and immature a man is, the harder it is for him to handle rejection, even if he did end the relationship. The signs of this are often anger, defensiveness, aggressive vocabulary or emotional blackmail. A typical example of such a reaction is where a man has realized that a woman has flawlessly moved on to a stage in her life where she no longer idolizes or needs him. Because admiration from a woman is so important to an emotionally immature man, he might get angry or become abusive during initial contact with his ex-girlfriend. Here's a typical exchange:

"Well, I know I made a decision to break-up with you, but you left me with no choice because you were always on my case and I didn't appreciate that really. You don't know how that made me feel, all you ever cared about is yourself!"

He clearly still blames his ex-girlfriend for the break-down of the relationship, which effectively means that there are elements of resentment and anger, but he is also showing clear signs of still not being able to let go. Do you really want to get back into the same arguments, situations and habit of blaming each other? Your ex might have made the initial move to get back in contact, but when you realize that he is not ready to acknowledge his actions or let go of the past, you should stay well clear of him.

When he is abusive and proceeds to call you names, hang up the phone. There is no need to excuse your actions, you don't need to put up with verbal abuse from anybody, EVER. The reason he is aggressive is because he is devastated that you have moved on. Quietly, he probably blames himself, but if he is controlling and wants to manipulate you he will still work to get you to accept responsibility. You would be surprised to know how many men manipulate and control their current women or exes that way.

Lastly, if a man contacts you on social networking sites, don't answer! If he asks to be your friend (again) on Facebook, don't react. If he starts following you on Twitter, don't follow him back. Beware of accepting a 'friends request' from him, because it can be applications or other software importing email contacts, therefore it might not even have anything to do with him (imagine the embarrassment if you accepted!). Besides, him being your Facebook friend means he will be able to track your movements and actions, which is not something you want to make easy for him. A serious man would never behave like teenager, he should therefore choose the first form of contact with you wisely.

CHAPTER 27

HOW TO ACT WHEN YOU MEET HIM FOR THE FIRST TIME SINCE THE BREAK-UP

Remind him about the old, surprise him with the new

When you arrange to meet your ex for the first time in weeks or months since the break-up, you are bound to feel anxious. The fact that you are agreeing to meet him means that you are considering having him back in your life and you probably want everything to go perfectly. However, you have to remember that it is not your first date with him, and that you need to silence the butterflies in your stomach and stay grounded. There is no better way to make him feel terrible about the break-up (trust me, you are not there to make him feel good and comfortable!) than to look as gorgeous as ever. You don't have to blow a fortune on a new outfit or a pair of new shoes, but what you absolutely must do is to be as polished and glamorous as possible.

Have your hair washed and apply products to make

it look shiny. There is nothing more sexy than a woman's lustrous hair and men absolutely love it. Spend some time on your personal grooming. Your nails must be clean and preferably varnished, and if you are wearing sandals, pay the same attention to your feet and toes. If the weather is nice and you are showing a bit of flesh, consider a little spray tan, but beware of automated booths that can produce disastrous results. Always seek a beauty therapist to apply a spray tan with a hand-held gun. With a subtle glow you not only look healthier, but also slimmer and younger. If you want to dazzle him with an amazing smile, treat yourself to a tooth whitening session. Have to look on eBay to find very cheap and effective alternatives to the expensive laser treatments offered by private clinics.

While you are deciding on what to wear, consider that you should look glamorous and classy, yet effortless, so be sure to stick to a reliable style that suits you. Don't choose today to try a brand new pair of high heels or experiment with a different style make-up. Consider putting on an item of clothing he has previously complimented, or one that you wore during a momentous occasion you two shared. By doing so, you are instantly bringing back good memories. However, accessorize the old piece with something new. You need to send a clear message with your outfit that your life has changed AND you have changed, which will keep him on his toes and interested. The whole point of making an effort, is to show him how beautiful you look when you are just being yourself, and how strong and confident you are.

If during the time you were apart from him you got a tattoo or changed the color of your hair, for example, don't panic that he isn't going to like it. If you had your ears pierced, wear a pair of amazing earrings, and make sure they are visible so he notices. Don't think that you ought to change your hair back to blonde if, after the split, you became a sexy brunette. All you need to do is to have your hair shiny and well blow-dried just to see him staring in amazement as you walk in! If you got a new tattoo and it is in a place where it can easily be seen, like your wrist for example, play with your hand to make sure he notices it. You may ask why I'm telling you to flaunt these things, the answer is simple: by displaying the changes that took place in you or your appearance within the time he chose to make himself scarce, you are showing him that you were not just sitting at home crying over him. Every little change in your appearance means you weren't wasting your time, that you wanted to break free from the past, and didn't think twice when it came to making these changes. It means you didn't care if he'd approve or not, because you were not considering him.

Don't go over old ground

The last thing you want when you and he finally meet for the first time in weeks or months is to have an argument. If this were to happen, you can be sure that you will never see him again, and the progress that you have made will be ruined. Some women feel they have got over the pain associated with the break-up and no longer feel anger towards their exes, but when they see them in person it all comes back to them, and suddenly it becomes obvious that they were not ready to face the situation yet. If this happens, the only thing you absolutely must do is control your emotions, because the fact you are still feeling resentment is no excuse for causing a scene and being branded unstable. Also, if you recognize that you feel that way, you can make your excuses and leave saying: "You know what, this wasn't such a good idea after all." After making such statement, grab your stuff and swiftly leave. Don't worry about his reaction. Nobody can force you to socialize with them if you don't want to and trust me, this is a much better exit than the one that ends in a heated argument!

However, even if the conversation with your ex flows and you are both having a good time, beware of reminiscing over the past. Reliving past scenarios, even in the most innocent of ways, can lead to a bad situation being brought up, which, in turn, may lead to tension. Never go back over old arguments - period! Yes, the chances are he might have changed his mind about something you two strongly disagreed about before, but if that's the case, he will tell you that himself when the time is right. For example:

"You know, I've thought long and hard about that...(situation). And now I've had some time on my own, I think you were actually right..."

If you revisit the old battlefields, chances are you might end up saying stuff like:

"Well, we wouldn't have split if not for your...(name the issue). So, are you still dead set on the idea?"

What do you think his answer will be? I'm thinking, the exact opposite of what you want to hear! It would also underline the fact that you two split up for a reason, and it should stay that way. However, if you're relaxed and he comes up with positive, acknowledging statements, you can just sit back and enjoy the benefits of your hard graft. You have given him space to realize what's important and where he had gone wrong, and he has done just that. Isn't that true love? Some certainly think so! So if he says anything that required maturity to work out, give a little. You don't need to admit you were wrong when it comes to anything from the past, if you are not ready to do so or don't think that you were, but acknowledging his efforts is important, so you may add something along the lines of:

"Perhaps, I could have handled it better too."

This doesn't actually mean you were wrong, but are acknowledging his efforts and giving a little too. Knowing that you now have control over emotions that drove you mad before is empowering, so use it wisely.

Now he has seen how gorgeous you look and that you can control situations you were perhaps unable to before, he will be reassured that it was the right move to contact you and see you again. The only way is up!

Act like a lady

When you finally see your ex after all the time you spent apart, allow him to lead you as if you two were dancing a tango. Even if you were the one to wear the trousers in your relationship, right now it should be his time to impress you. If he was the kind of boyfriend who relied on you to make decisions (everything from the restaurant or bar choice, to what he drank or ate while you were there), quite literally force him to make an effort and invite you somewhere out of his own initiative. If you hear him say: "So where are we going?", simply answer: "I will leave the choice to you." By doing so, you are letting him know that you are inviting him to take initiative, which is something that he has to learn to do from now on, in order to win you back.

If you have tendencies to talk a lot and dominate conversations, you need to drill it into your head this can't happen now. Sometimes the intense monologue (yes, you are actually having a conversation with yourself most of the time as you are not allowing anyone to join in!), is just a side-effect of being nervous. Control your emotions, and if you need to take herbal remedies before you see him to calm down, do so. If drinking alcohol stimulates you in an undesirable ways, be sure to opt out of your usual glass of wine and order a soda.

The best thing you can do during your first meeting is to allow him to talk and listen carefully to what he has to say. Concentrating on his words is important. Don't be afraid of an uncomfortable silence and don't try to fill up the gaps. It is the person who listens who controls the conversation, not the other way round. There is no better way to judge whether he is worth another go than to listen to him. If he relies on you to take charge of most of the conversation, don't make it easy for him. He needs to treat you like a lady, so it is down to him to entertain you. If he was used to you talking non-stop, he will have something of a shock to see that you can be calm and composed. It will also put pressure on him, because he'll need to step up to make the date entertaining and interesting.

When it's time to call it a day, allow him to pick up the bill, but do offer to pay half. Make sure it is never the over way round! I know so many women who pay for their men and then complain that they don't treat them like ladies. Truth is, they are not allowing them to do so. Perhaps you were guilty of that yourself in the relationship with your ex, so now is the time to show him that that part of you is also well and truly gone. If he is not asking for the bill and you need to go, leave half the money on the table. Watch his reaction. It's not about the money really; it's about him treating you like a lady. If he doesn't offer to pay fully, don't go out with him again. He should be the one trying to impress you after all and part of it is paying for you. This doesn't mean paying for you non-stop from now on, but that first meeting after weeks or months is important, and he should be the one making all the effort. Picking up the bill is definitely acting in a mature manner.

Be mysterious

When you are with him, whether you are dining in a restaurant or having a picnic in the park, keep eye contact and a mysterious smile as much as you can. You want to keep him guessing as to what you are thinking in order to keep him interested. You want him to realize that the person sitting in front of him has the very best traces of his ex-girlfriend, and the amazing qualities of a hot, new woman he is just getting to know.

Be sure to keep eye contact throughout the time you are with him. Don't do it in a provocative way, but as if you are hanging on to his every word and giving him attention. Lean forward slightly when you talk to him, subtly not aggressively. Listen to him, interact, be interested in what he says, ask questions, but don't interrupt him. React immediately and appropriately to what he says. Laugh when something is funny, commiserate with him on sad news, but keep a slight distance to everything and don't give away too much of what you are thinking. Run your fingers through your hair and act in a feminine manner. Be relaxed and receptive.

If there were changes that took place in your life during his absence, don't completely dominate the conversation talking about them or anything else related only to you, your career, your friends, etc. Get the balance right, always ask about him first and WAIT for when he asks you about your life in return. When he does, tell him about a promotion at work or a new project you are working on, but keep it brief. If he doesn't ask about anything related to you, you may safely assume he is not that interested in you and you don't need to produce any information.

When you need to go, don't say what you're up to next. Avoid doing this:

"Got to go, I need to see my friend Laura tonight, then I'm going to do some food shopping and then catch up on some sleep."

If you two got on great, he will have you on his mind after you part. There are two variations on what he will now be contemplating:

"It was great to see her, she looked fantastic, I'm glad I know she is with her friend now and doing food shopping later."

Or:

"She looked fantastic, I wonder what she is doing now? I hope she's not meeting another guy later!"

Mysterious women have fascinated men for thousands of years; just look at the portrait of the Mona Lisa. If you give away too much of what you are thinking and what you are, or were, doing since the split, you have given him all the information he could have pondered about too early. Remember that he contacted you because he hadn't heard from you for ages, and is now curious to know what you have been doing, and are doing. Too many women make the mistake of providing men with too much information. Be sure to know that your life doesn't need broadcasting to him or anyone else. If you feel the need to do so, perhaps you should consider that you are an attention seeker and ask yourself why. If you leave no aura of mystery after the first meeting, don't expect his level of interest in you to be very high.

Never arrive too early to meet him

When you are about to see your ex for the first time in a long while, be sure that you are setting the right impression from the beginning and never arrive too early and be seen waiting. It is his and only his job to be waiting for you! Anyone can be late due to traffic or other unforeseen circumstances, so your safest bet is to schedule your arrival around 20 minutes later than expected. That way, if your ex is ten minutes late, he still needs to wait for you for another ten minutes. If your ex is more than half an hour late, don't wait for him a minute longer - even if you are dying to see him and made considerable effort with your looks. I know it's frustrating but wherever you are, exit the premises swiftly and grab a cab or a bus home, even if he is just around the corner. It will teach him that your time is precious and you have far more important things to do than wait for him to appear. Later on, if you see that he is regretful and apologizes, you can grant him another chance of seeing you, but make it no sooner than a further two weeks away. If he made you wait 30 minutes, for example, make him wait three weeks to see you, and so on. If he gets the hump, let him be grumpy, don't entertain it with your time or attention. Don't explain yourself either because he is the one who should be doing that. Let's just be clear that if a man is super-keen to see a woman he will re-arrange everything he has to in order to see her. You know the score yourself, because I am sure that you re-arranged your commitments few times in order to see him before. If he wants to be there on time he will also find a way. The more he is looking forward to seeing you, the more he will want to be there on time.

Establish if there is still connection

You may think that it's obvious - otherwise he wouldn't have contacted you, appeared and be sat right in front of you - but be sure to detect if there's still chemistry between you two. I have known women to presume there is, only to find out that their exes have decided otherwise.

In order to establish what effect you have on him, pay attention to how your ex reacts to you. Notice his reaction when you walk in and approach him. Does he get up to greet you? Is he concentrating on you and only you? Do you see that he can't take his eyes of you? Do you notice him hanging on to your every word? Is he interested in what you are saying and backs it up with appropriate reactions and questions? If that's the case you can assume that he is very interested in you, and if you feel the same way about him it's a good sign. If you don't see that you have made a great impression on him after you have walked in, if he is looking elsewhere while you are talking to him and can barely keep up eye contact with you, or is fiddling with his phone for example, start preparing your exit. When I say 'preparing', it shouldn't take you longer than five minutes to be out. It doesn't demand any explanation. Pick up your stuff, say: "Well, I have to go now," and be off! Bear in mind that this is extremely unlikely, but should you experience this, know that acting in this way when he wanted to see you means he is an asshole who doesn't deserve to hear your voice again!

To sum up what we've just said, when your ex gets in touch, it is only you who holds the power to what happens next! So, no need to feel anxious or nervous. If you apply what we have just covered in dealing with him, you will soon find out about his real intentions towards you. It might not be what you wanted it to be, but at least then you'll know not to hang on to a man who will eventually humiliate you again and cause you more heartache.

However, if it is good news and you manage to work things out, consider that your new relationship will be much stronger and more loving than ever before. I know a woman who after getting dumped by her boyfriend managed to turn the tables, and now, after ten years together, he is thanking his lucky stars that he is back with her! And it took him a year to get back in touch with her! Every situation, every person, the circumstances surrounding the relationship and the break-up are so different. The key is to act with self-love and dignity; it will never let you down.

PART 5

NOT GETTING BACK TOGETHER

CHAPTER 28

UNDERSTANDING WHY HE STILL HASN'T CALLED

Some men are so stubborn and masochistic that they will think nothing of making themselves suffer, or depriving themselves from a loving relationship, for the sake of not giving you what you want. Others are in denial and just waiting for you to call them. Some prefer to fantasize about you every day and night instead of facing reality. There are some who think that they can teach you a lesson by not getting in contact, while others are simply too scared to do so. Whatever the reason, if you hoped for your ex to get in touch and he still hasn't, it is not always the case that he has forgotten you, in fact it could be quite the opposite really.

Some men just don't know the right way of initiating contact

When at the end of your relationship things fell apart, it was either you or he who finished it. Perhaps the break-up was quite sudden and it took you both by surprise. Perhaps words were spoken that might be difficult to take back. Regardless of the reason for a split, consider that even after a few months have passed, your ex might still have feelings for you and want you back, but might be finding it difficult to initiate contact. In other words, he might not know the right way of doing it. He might be protecting himself from humiliation, as he doesn't know what you are thinking and feeling. He may not want to overwhelm you. He may not want to disturb your life balance. You are still on his mind quite a lot and it may go either way. So what's next? It should be him who comes to you, so still don't initiate contact. If he realizes that he wants to be with you, he will eventually find a way.

Some are just stubborn

As I mentioned at the beginning, some men are so incredibly stubborn that they will act in a masochistic way just to spite you. Truth is, the people they are hurting the most are themselves. Stubborn people are the hardest to deal with in relationships, because they are completely uncompromising. In relationships they tend to look out only for themselves and barely see their partner's point of view. They will always act in a defensive manner and never acknowledge their mistakes - even if they are obvious. If your ex is a stubborn man, he might be thinking that you ought to do the running and fixing of the relationship, because he can't accept his own part in the break-up. He might be waiting for you to react and gratify his ego. What's next? Nothing! It's like not wearing gloves in the winter while your hands are freezing cold only because someone's telling you to wear them. Do you want to waste your energy on him? If he doesn't call – you've had a lucky escape.

Some don't want to change

If you dumped a man because of his unreasonable behavior and are maintaining no contact, he knows that you mean business and you won't accept anymore nonsense. While he might still be very much hooked on you, or even in love with you, before anything can happen, he needs time to re-evaluate his life. This is not an easy process and requires him to be in 'no man's land' for a while to give himself a proper reality check. You may find that he enjoys his lifestyle too much to change it to suit a relationship with you. You may also find he will realizes that his life is empty without you. What do you do until then? Nothing. If you contact him first you are as good as accepting his conditions of a relationship, because you are showing him you can't live without him. He needs to reappear on his own accord - after he's realized that you won't lift a finger to get him back if things remain the same. If he doesn't call, your answer is: you were never that important to him and you two were never meant to be.

Some don't want to risk another defeat

He still loves you but he might be reluctant to give it another go because you have tried and failed before. Or maybe he is simply very emotional still about the relationship and doesn't want to take the risk of feeling the pain of the break-up again. He is either not over you, or perhaps even a woman from his past who has caused him emotional turmoil. This might have been traumatic for him and the current situation may be opening up old wounds. If he is willing to pass on the opportunity of a relationship with someone he still loves because of fear, he needs professional help rather than a girlfriend. What do you do? As much as it is frustrating, you have to let him be. He won't act any differently if you corner him or come forward and tell him that you still love him. Some traumatized men end up lonely and alone because they can't shake off their fear or the past. You are not a head doctor. Let someone else do the hard work.

Some are in denial

This may be true immediately after the break-up, but for some it lasts for a long time afterwards too. His denial might worsen when he sees you with another man! He might still be thinking that one day you'll be back together, but he is not actively taking steps to make it happen. He's living in a fantasy land where he doesn't have to accept that the relationship ended, so therefore doesn't have to deal with the break-up pain. He also doesn't have to face up to the truth about his part in the failed relationship. And now he doesn't see that he has to do any work to get you back either. Living in denial means not being brutally honest with himself and not acknowledging anything. How do you get him out of it? You can't. You can only live your own reality, you can't tell others how to live theirs. He may or may not wake up one day and act to get you back. But don't waste your life and wait for him to do so. It's far from being a safe bet.

Some are sex addicts

If your ex was a serial cheat, consider that he might be addicted to sexual encounters with other women. Being a serial cheat is an addiction like any other and in this case it comes from low self-esteem. It's a quick high that doesn't last very long. It's an issue that he has to solve for himself. Not everyone is prepared to admit they have a problem and not everyone is prepared to work to get rid of it. He may still have feelings for you, but like everything else, he has to choose to work on his issues himself and then choose you.

Some are scared of reaction of friends and family

It's great to have role models and take inspiration from people, but when the influence of others stretches as far as being fearful of their reaction on our life choices, you know it has gone too far. Some men are so strongly influenced by their friends and family, especially if you haven't managed to make great impression on them, that they will go as far as not contacting you and denying themselves a second chance with you just to avoid upsetting their nearest and dearest. Yes, he is Mr. Doormat and he will never change! Even if he eventually plucks up the courage to give the relationship with you another go, he will still be beating himself up about justifying it to his family or friends (or both). He may ask you to keep it a secret. Truth is, the people around him are really bullies, but he is unlikely to see that. Is this the kind of man you really want to spend your life with? If you were to get back with him there would be resentment and anger that he can't handle himself. Every woman deserves a mature man, not someone who acts like a child.

Some are narcissistic and are waiting for you to make the first step

Are you shocked? Don't be, because some men think they are so special that women should be chasing after them and pursuing them. Regardless of who initiated the break-up, these men think that it is down to you to make contact and declare your feelings. These men have massive egos, but why do they think they are that special? Well, women who get desperate and try to fix their relationships with them provide them with attention they don't deserve, and they wrongly translate it into them thinking they are God's gift to women. Don't become a victim of his game playing and power struggle - because essentially this is what it is all about. Don't give him the satisfaction! These men don't respect or even remember the women who were crazy about them, and they've probably never had the chance or the opportunity to find out what's it like to be on the receiving side of such treatment. Incidentally, this is the easiest type to lure back into your arms with the no contact rule. Shock him. Make him feel he is not so special after all. *Ignore the man to get the man!*

Some are in other relationships you were not aware of

This may sound absolutely awful but it happens more often than you think. A man splits from a woman because she is dangerously close to finding out that he is leading a double life. Or he can no longer sustain a double life and has no choice but to let go. Then, he never calls. You wonder what happened. Living a fantasy life (and a lie) is a way of escaping his everyday dull reality. A man can have a long- term partner who is stable and dependable, but misses the adventurous part of the relationship. He may get involved with someone new who is unaware and unsuspecting of his other arrangements. He may even fall head-over-hills with that person. But when it comes to picking reality over fantasy, the former has to take priority. He is unlikely to come clean and reveal the situation to both women - because he would most likely lose both. What is he to do? Break up with an unsuspecting woman and often make up false reasons to back up his decision, that's what he will do. He will be lonely and suffering, but he won't get in touch because he simply can't.

Some are still angry

Despite all you did, he remains angry at you about the break-up, but he could not be angry if he didn't care. Anger passes with time, so do feelings. Unfortunately, the chances are he won't get in touch while he still feels this way and by the time those feelings pass, he might not have the same amount of love for you left. If he still loves you and you love him can this be fixed? If you weren't able to communicate without anger before, you are unlikely to go forward. If he can let go of his negativity and approach you without anger, you may be able to give it another go. If he contacts you but still showcases anger, he isn't ready to talk yet. He is the one who has to make it happen, not you.

Some are going through other serious things and haven't got around to dealing with the break-up yet

This may sound a little harsh, you may say: "When he broke up with me, I couldn't have felt any worse, even if at the same time I'd lost my job, my house and my cat died!" Unfortunately that's not what reality is all about, and the only person who may think that way is one who has no experience of the above. Financial difficulties, business or work related issues, housing problems and many others have a severely draining affect on anyone at the best of times. If they happen around the same time the break-up occurs, it may delay the reaction to the loss of a partner and subsequently postpone the break-up pain. If something has already happened you can't go trying to fix the break-up while everything else is collapsing around you; you attend to that first. His main responsibility may be rescuing his business from going under or continuing with an important commitment he had undertaken. He will eventually get to realize that he is single and will have to deal with the emotions then. This one requires your patience.

Some are scared of rejection

Fear of rejection remains the most common reason a man does not get in touch if he still has strong feelings for you. Also, the more immature he is, the harder it is for him to overcome it. He will be actively talking himself out of contacting you because he doesn't want to be faced with the possibility of you telling him you do not care anymore, or are in a different relationship. But if that's not the case and you really want him to contact you, can you prompt him? It's not advisable to do so. If he cares he will still come forward. On the contrary, if he was arrogant and dumped you, you should get a little satisfaction from this, because now he understands what he has put you through. He will come to you if that's what he truly wants.

Some want to do a 'Great Gatsby'

Who doesn't know the story about Jay Gatsby by F Scott Fitzgerald? A man besotted with a beautiful woman pretends to be a rich, eligible bachelor, and when he finally reveals that he is poor and can't provide for her he gets dumped, but makes it his life's priority to gain wealth and power in order to get her back later in life. Does this happen in real life? If we were to translate it into modern times, it would be the classic story of wrong timing. Some relationships may end because people decide to move to another country to grow professionally, or to obtain different qualifications, or perhaps because they have to remain focused on their current job and have no time for a serious partner. Some are forced with difficult choices where circumstances dictate they opt out of a relationship. It may be the case of - not now, but maybe some time later in life. They may never forget you, and as their circumstances change, they may reappear in your life. The key is not to expect it. But it might happen.

Finally... some are assholes who never appreciated you

It doesn't give me any pleasure to say this, but your ex may have been one of them. Your friends may confirm this. The stories others tell about him may confirm this. If you know his ex-girlfriend she may confirm this. His behavior towards you while you were in a relationship with you may confirm this. The way he broke up with you may confirm this. More importantly, if your intuition tells you that

that's the case, listen to it carefully, it might just be telling you the truth.

Why is a man like that not worth waiting for a phone call from? Because there is a good chance that he didn't share your feelings or involvement in the relationship. Also that he wasn't into you the way you were in to him, and that he treated you casually or like a stepping stone to someone else. Of course it hurts to even think about it, but it is no good to live in denial. He wasn't the caring, loving partner you thought he was. It's hard to accept harsh reality, but if you don't face up to it you will as good as waiting for the boogeyman to re-appear. When you come to terms with reality you are allowing yourself to start the healing process. You deserve better, and in a way he has done you a favor, because going through a break-up and perhaps reading this book you are beginning to realize your true value. You will be smarter now and never allow any other man to take advantage. That makes you strong and wiser than him. With time you will wonder what the hell you saw in him. It will happen!

CHAPTER 29

HOW TO HANDLE THE NEWS THAT YOUR EX STARTED DATING

It takes a long time and strong discipline to get over someone who we still care about, especially when we find they have moved on. You may feel that you have completely healed, but finding out about him dating someone else may reopen the wounds in a very intense way.

When you are told your ex is seeing someone while you hoped and prayed for him to get back with you, you sink to levels of despair you may not known you had in you. You feel betrayed – even though you are no longer together – so technically he isn't doing anything wrong. Still, you can't and don't want to picture it in your head, let alone accept it as reality. This is such a difficult one to handle, I know because I've been there. But, if only for a moment, and with a clear head, you could think about it without emotions - you'd find that it doesn't actually change your situation at all - it might be exactly what you need to get over him in record time.

How to remain dignified when he dates first

If someone tells you about him dating or you have found out from other sources like Facebook, regardless of how shocked, angry and hurt you are, don't show it! DON'T GIVE HIM THE SATISFACTION! Don't ever leave angry or disrespectful comments on Facebook and other social networking sites. Don't email or text him demanding to know if it's true or asking for explanation. Don't ever make desperate phone calls. He will probably not answer anyway, because he will have a fair idea what's it all about.

A man always expects his ex to cause a scene after she finds out he has moved on and started dating. He is prepared for it. What he doesn't expect is for you to keep your cool and ignore it. That's what he is completely unprepared for. He wants you to make a silly, desperate phone call and even better that you make it while his new squeeze is around. It totally magnifies his importance if women cry for his love and attention and show they can't get over him. He thinks: "Wow, that makes me look pretty amazing in my new girlfriend's eyes!"

I don't know about you, but I would personally prefer to get someone to tie my hands for fear of slipping up and calling him. I would rather cry into my pillow for a fortnight, but still never show a tear in public. I would rather walk my dog with toothpaste smeared all over my face than for him to find out his actions bother me! Look, it's hard, super-hard even. But it's a bit like with the break-up itself - the initial shock will wear off. It's not easy to nurture that thought, but you will eventually accept it. Try not to think about it and concentrate on yourself instead. I know it sounds completely unrealistic, but trust me it's doable. Keep your mind occupied with other things. Get busy. If you know the woman he's dating be careful not to talk about your pain in front of someone who may know her too. Generally remain tightlipped about the whole thing unless you are talking to really close friends of yours. I know I have said this before, but I really want to drive it home: don't contact him about it! Refrain from giving into temptation to call and ask him: "Why her?" You don't want to know the answer and the bottom line is - you don't need it. It's over anyway. If you two were meant to be or were happy together you would still be together. You split up for a reason and let it stay that way. Realize that moving on and starting to date other people after the break-up is a fact of life. Help yourself by re-reading the list of negative traits about him. When you're done and based on his negative aspects, ask yourself, is he the kind of man you dreamed about settling down with as a little girl? He hasn't changed a bit just because he is with someone else; he is still the same person.

Don't be jealous either about his new woman,

because whatever problem you have mentioned on that list, she will now endure. Fact! Take a deep breath and re-read the part of this book where I talk about taking steps to protect yourself from making a panic phone call. On the contrary, appreciate the fact that once you are ready to date and news will spread about you going out with someone, your ex will be feeling exactly the same, while you might hardly be able to remember his name.

Finally, learn from some of the most successful women of our times. Can you imagine the pain felt by Demi Moore when she found out about her ex, Ashton Kutcher's new relationship with the beautiful and much younger actress Mila Kunis? Media all over the world were reporting that she was devastated to the point of checking herself into rehab. However weeks later she emerged looking healthier and stronger than ever. And when Jude Law cheated on gorgeous Sienna Miller with his children's nanny - who later sold her story to the tabloids - the actress and fashion icon was pictured enjoying a party with family and friends. And when David Beckham's alleged affair with Spanish model Rebecca Loos was broadcasted in media all over the world, his wife Victoria was being photographed waving to paparazzi while skiing in the French Alps with her family and - her husband.

I don't know about you, but I have a strong suspicion that none of these women were particularly in the right mood to party or appear in public looking super-happy. But by doing so they did not allow themselves to be portrayed as victims. They took charge of their lives in very difficult circumstances and decided to get through it with their heads held high. It's a choice and you can make it too. More importantly; *you can stick to it.*

You are stronger than you give yourself credit for

Consider that this break-up and all the feelings that accompany it could mean the re-birth of you. Also that as painful as it seems - the beginning of a very special year for you. Here's what I want you to tell yourself, repeat after me:

This is my year of honesty - be honest with yourself about your current life situation. Are you otherwise happy, despite the break-up? Maybe you need to make decisions to find happiness that is within your reach, but you are stopping yourself from doing so. Do you need help with making these decisions? Perhaps you have got to deal with your own fears? Quit lying to yourself. Not only when it comes to relationships, but apply it to other areas of your life. For example, if you are a dress size 16 - don't buy clothes that are size 14 because you can't deal with the fact you think you should be thinner. You can't get motivated to apply changes in your life unless you know what you need to do to change things for the better. So make that first step of being brutally honest with yourself. Subsequently be honest with others too. Don't accept pity and don't offer advice based on pity. Become a better, stronger you. The answers lie within you.

This is my year of commitment - and by commitment I mean commitment to yourself and your life choices. Nothing is more important than pursuing your own happiness. Once you have identified what *you* want and need (not your ex), relentlessly go after it. You only live once, and whatever you gain is yours to use and enjoy to your, and only your, advantage. If you have identified that you are not happy with your career for example - but are feeling that you can't make any changes in that department due to inadequate education or skills - your priority should be with fixing that. Commitment to ourselves is being passionate about ourselves, and that's what draws others to us. It shows self-love and self-respect.

This is my year of freedom - you are a free agent and there are some fantastic benefits of being single. Really! Just enjoy not having to consult anyone about your food shopping, choosing a holiday destination, home decoration, deciding what time you get home, what you will wear, not sharing your bed, being able to flirt with whoever you want and date them, being able to spend your money on yourself thus avoiding unnecessary expenditure like your ex's birthday, Christmas and Valentine's presents, for example. I know I have said all of this before, but I really want to make sure you realize this. Separating from an ex also means that you no longer have to put up with the struggle of your past relationship. You can let go of the arguments, anger, resentment, jealousy, despair, feeling unfulfilled, rejected, abandoned, unappreciated and taken for granted. Consider how many women all over the world are going through it as we speak - but YOU are already free!

This is my year of new beginnings - out with the old; in with the new, should be your new motto. This is the time to break off old routines and kill off things that take up your time but are not beneficial to you in any way. Are you learning a new skill? Have you thought about doing something like piercing your ears for years, but only done it recently? Or have you decided to take time off work and travel abroad? Anything new that will enrich you or provide you with new experiences is beneficial and shows that you are bravely pursuing your new life.

This is my year of progress - if the relationship with your ex turned out to be a big waste of time, this is the year to devote to really moving forward with your life. Perhaps you thought that your ex was 'the one' and were already making plans to settle down? Well, life has another plan for you and you don't know what that is yet, which is in itself exciting. By refusing to dwell on your past and continuing going forward in life, you are truly opening up the path to your future.

This is my year of opportunity - and you will not miss it because you are stuck with an unsuitable partner or in the past anymore. You may have postponed or refused good things that knocked your door while you were with him, because you were considering the effect on your relationship. You might have turned down the chance of promotion, long-haul foreign travel, exciting projects and many other things, but now, no one stands in your way to new adventures. Treat everything as a blessing and use it wisely.

This is my year of security - your security comes from your independence, peace of mind and being at ease with yourself, because there is no one draining your energy anymore. When you take a moment, think about how much more secure you feel without that volatile relationship, where you never knew if you were coming or going. Being secure increases your self-esteem and that in turn draws men to you like bees to honey. Security means independence and not relying on anyone. It is self-sufficiency which is truly priceless - because you don't have to put up with any man just because he is providing material or emotional comfort.

This is my year of decisions - and the first good decision you have made is to cut your ex out of your life despite him still being in your heart. Decision-making is a sign of maturity. Making decisions is not an easy or stress-free process, and it almost doesn't matter what the outcome is, just as long as you can decide on something and stick to it. That's the difficult part. Purposely avoiding making difficult (or simple) decisions is a sign of cowardness. Trying to get others to make a decision for us is like asking them to live our lives for us. Yet lots of people live their lives that way, all over the world, everyday. If you were not a confident decision maker before, take this opportunity to get better at it; it's your life. Empower yourself by deciding your own fate. You don't want to wake up as a 70-year-old and realize that you lived someone else's dream. This is the time to make it happen!

This is my year of clarity - clarity comes from being honest with yourself and seeing every situation for what it truly is. Clarity is being realistic and that comes from acceptance. When you were in the relationship with your ex, you were perhaps not seeing things for what they truly were. Perhaps he clouded your judgment with his opinions, actions and promises. Maybe you needed time out or no contact to regain your own individual, clear vision. Now that you got here again, you can appreciate that a clear mind means no one can play you or use you again - because you are too smart to let them do so.

This is my year of learning - and we learn every single day of our lives until we die. It's just that some people care to notice and get wiser, and some never learn a single lesson and fall into the same traps over and over again. Well, you will not be single for a very long time. But before you set off back into the big, bad world of dating, you have to remember what this experience has taught you about yourself and men. Don't fall into the same patterns - they haven't worked before and they will definitely not work in the future. If you always fall in love with hopeless, unavailable men – don't do it to yourself anymore - avoid them! If you give any man who waves his hand in the air the luxury of your time, attention, affection, your body and mind, etc, without making him work for it, be prepared to suffer all over again. You now know what will happen and it's your choice not to repeat history. Don't become too easily available and don't let anyone control you. These are just examples. You know exactly what standards you have to maintain.

This is my year of fulfillment - it's high time you were rewarded for your hard work. Whether it's work or other areas of your life, once you have a grip on it, you are unbreakable and unstoppable. The first reward should come from you, to you. You have managed to shake off the bad relationship and are heading for better things in life.

This is my year of empowerment - and finally, once equipped with all knowledge, motivation and self-respect, consider that everything happens for a reason. Think how much you have actually gained from being with your ex and then breaking up with him and experiencing heartbreaking and, at times, terrifying emotions. Consider that it was worth it if only to learn what NOT to do again. And while you are contemplating this, amongst many other things, realize that you might just be… over him.

PART 6

LEARNING FROM YOUR BREAK-UP

CHAPTER 30

IF MEN LOVE SWEETHEARTS, WHY DO THEY MARRY BITCHES?

Here comes arguably one of the biggest sources of confusion in the dating world: if men are so certain they love women who are sweethearts, how come they settle for bitches to spend their lives with? The answer is so simple it is almost ridiculous. Here it comes: men think that bitches are sweethearts! Why? Because they are being played by them to think that way. Some also go out with women who don't give a toss about them, so they don't show any emotions, which men confuse for support!

I've never read the best selling Sherry Argov book: *Why Men Marry Bitches*. My own conclusions on the subject are formed from my own experiences, listening to my readers and women I talked to when I was collecting material for my case studies for *It Really Is All His Fault*.

To make it more understandable for you, let me ask

you: for how many men in your life have you been an exemplary girlfriend, and how many of them broke up with you? How much time do you devote to a man when you are in a relationship with him? Do you cook and dress to impress him? How many times have you dropped your friends like a couple of hot potatoes to spend time with your man? I will go further and ask you: have you ever cancelled your own plans to accommodate your partners? Have you ever wrapped yourself in his life so completely that you stopped recognizing your own needs and prioritized his? Have you ever praised him for his sexual performance when you knew it was rather average? Finally, do answer if the above situations have caused you to feel anger and resentment, because it seems that no matter what you did, he seemed to be slipping away emotionally anyway and had less and less respect for you – is that right?

If you answered "Yes" to a few of these questions, I will tell you that you are a sweetheart, but to a man you may appear as a bitch too, because he sees you as being constantly on his back and creating pressure for him. Yes, your intentions are pure and you do want what's best for him - but men can't be tamed that way. They need to learn the hard way. When you accommodate a man and support him, he takes you for granted. When you let him get on with his life and stop being interested in him (literally!) he thinks you are relaxed and supportive and are not putting pressure on him. A year ago, when I was still in the relationship with my ex, he told me about his friend's girlfriend - who he repeatedly called a 'sweetheart'. My ex also didn't spare her other praise. She was apparently 'calm, supportive, relaxed, fair...', in other words - all the things I was not. I thought, as someone who loved my boyfriend, I ought to care that he eats well and doesn't get sick, works less and spends more time relaxing. I didn't like it when he travelled abroad for work because I missed him very much. My boyfriend saw that as me trying to control him and pull him away from his work. 'The sweetheart' didn't cook for her boyfriend, 'because she didn't restrict him'. She was extremely happy for him to go abroad because she always tagged along and went to places she wouldn't have had a chance to go to otherwise. She didn't mind that he worked long hours, because she was driving him to achieve so she could photograph herself with him and somehow associate herself with his success. All for his own good of course! To all appearances, she was just an average woman, but still managed to keep her boyfriend wrapped around her little finger, so I guess, she was far from average when it came to playing him! The most amazing thing was to watch the game she played, and how her boyfriend and everyone else lapped this up. I, however, have another name for her: USER. Her boyfriend will probably end up marrying her, and let's just say it will be no more or less than he deserves.

Is it any wonder that men can be easily played? They

seem to lack basics when it comes to relationships and confuse being used for support. This seems the most offensive thing for a woman who genuinely cares for her partner and his wellbeing. For years I had been carrying my partner in my relationships, until I asked myself a question: how is this working for me? And this was a turning point in my life. Some good old advice, offered by my mum and gran, is that a woman should always be classy and love herself first. Trouble was, those words weren't striking a cord with me. Besides, we are always full of good advice for others, and just can't seem to apply it to ourselves. Until a moment comes, and it may well have been the departure of my ex, when I realised I had definitely had enough.

This is where I am going to try to convince you that you must, ABSOLUTELY MUST love yourself first to be with someone. No man will ever thank you for being too nurturing. You are not his mother and some of us women forget that. Nature made us nurturing, and we often bring this into our relationships. Remember to keep the balance by portraying yourself as priority at all times, though. Here's how to stay on the right track:

Don't ever just accommodate a man - Your needs come first - period! Don't even attempt to show your caring nature by showing how much you can do for him. Unless he is sick, disabled, is going through bereavement or has just become homeless, it is not up to you to help him with anything. Not only will he not thank you for anything, but will take you for granted.

Don't wait for him to make plans, make your own - If you are constantly waiting for him to make plans for the two of you to see each other in the evenings or do something at the weekends, you will keep all your free time open exclusively for him, and will miss out on the time spent with friends or on your own. Furthermore, you will start appearing as too available and he will become suspicious of your intentions. When things come too easy we become suspects! More about this in the next chapter.

Don't ever change your plans for him - If you were going to see friends and he cancels his plans last minute and declares he wants to spend an evening with you, don't even think of doing the same! Be firm and no matter how much you want to see him, stick to your original plan. If you drop everything to be with him, when you were only his second choice in the first place, he will always think of you as a backup plan. On the contrary, next time he will think twice before he makes plans that don't include you.

Never spend any money that you are not prepared to spend on yourself to buy presents for him - Here's a little example for you. For our first Christmas together, I bought my ex an expensive gift. Although it cost much more than I was prepared to spend on anyone else that

Christmas, I was more than happy to do it because I knew how much he would like it. Wanna know how it worked for me? He was happy with what I got him but didn't match the present either in gesture or in value. At the time, in his workshop, he was working on a commission that included wooden vases, so... I got one for Christmas! You would be right in guessing that the one I got, probably didn't pass his buyer's quality control; sad.

Don't advise him on his style - even if you think that he needs your advice BADLY. Every man wants to be himself, so just let him be. If you pursue this, he will feel resentful. If he is extra stubborn he will make an issue out of it, so don't do it. If he truly has such bad style, why date him in the first place? You may think he has 'looks or style potential', but you can't view real people in such a light.

Always wait for him to call or contact you - This is essential and crucial to your relationship with him. If you set the standard high from the beginning, you will never worry or pray for his phone call. Chase him from the beginning and be sure that he will keep running in the opposite direction as fast as he can. The choice is yours.

Be elusive and mysterious, ALWAYS! - If you don't allow yourself to remain a little mysterious, be sure that you will soon become boring in his eyes. Sure, we can't constantly surprise the people we are with, but if by the second date you've already told him your life story, what's left? If you don't reveal much, you will keep him guessing!

Loving yourself is not just an empty slogan. It takes practice. Not many women are born with it. In fact, it seems that the ones who were, are the proverbial sweethearts I described earlier. The true art of it though it to actually love someone while allowing yourself to be a priority. Forget about silly game playing. You have to first understand it and then believe it to live your life by that rule. If you are now single it is the perfect time to start making changes - so by the time your next relationship starts you will be a completely different person. Believe me, it is what will ultimately bring you to the man of your dreams. And, if your ex missed out, make sure that the next man in your life will not. Maintain your well-being as priority at all times, and pay little attention to his until he proves that he is worth it.

And on that subject, I can't resist telling one last story about my friend Evelina, whose boyfriend of six months broke up with her by text message from Australia. When he returned to London, he called to arrange a meeting with her to pass on her belongings. Before she went to meet him at Liverpool Street station, only God knows why, but she baked his favorite cake and took it with her to meet him. I remember her telling me that he looked at her as if she was crazy, and then he said with disbelief:

"I broke up with you and you are bringing me cake?"

"You always liked this cake!" she replied.

After he said good bye and they parted, she turned around to look at him one more time, just in perfect time to see him throw the cake in a waste bin in the street. Ahhhhh!

CHAPTER 31

HOW TO GET RESPECT FROM A FUTURE PARTNER BY SETTING BOUNDARIES AND STICKING TO THEM

If a relationship is going down a slippery slope, you have probably issued hundreds of empty threats by now that you are going to leave. Problem is, he will have stopped taking you seriously after the third threat. For the future and for the sake of your new relationship, with whoever that may be, your ex or someone completely different, you need to ensure an adequate level of respect. Therefore, you need to set boundaries to be able to know when enough is enough.

The first warning

First of all, when your man has made a mistake, don't write him off straight away. Whatever it is he has done, remember that as humans we all make mistakes. However, you need to make a decision whether to forgive him, and it is only you who can decide what you are able to forgive. As people and as women we are all very different. It may be acceptable for some of us to forgive a cheating boyfriend his betrayal, but for others the fact that they caught their boyfriend lying is a deal-breaker. As I said before, we are all different, we have varying standards and priorities, and it is not for other people to judge us, or for us to judge them. However, if you decide that the man you are with is worth it, you issue him with a verbal warning, meaning - you let him know exactly how you feel about whatever it is that he has done - and explain that you will not tolerate such behavior in the future. Don't threaten, be calm, say what you mean and mean what you say. You should make him understand that you did not appreciate whatever it is that he has done and why not.

The second warning

However, if the situation resurfaces, you have to be more firm. This means you have to make yourself even clearer about how much his behaviour has hurt you or upset you.

The final warning

If it happens again, there is no need to explain anything. He has heard it all before and knows the score. Next time; you're walking! And when it does happen again, you do just that. Because you absolutely cannot keep holding on to someone who continuously hurts you. And bottom line is, when someone does things to upset you, fully understanding how that makes you feel, they clearly don't respect you, and certainly can't love you. And by continuing to stay with such a person you give them the green light for such behavior.

CHAPTER 32

WHY ARE WE MASOCHISTS?

The answer is simple: because we want to believe that the person will change; because we imagine a future with them; because we idealize them or give them far more credit than they deserve. But by doing so, it's as good as giving them ammunition to load a gun and shoot it at the relationship. Your partner needs to know from very early on you have standards that you are not prepared to drop because he happened to grace your life with his presence. It is the only way of ensuring his growing respect for you. It is the only way of truly making him realize that you love yourself more than you love him - which will make him pursue you like crazy - no matter if you have been together a month or 15 years. Smart women understood a long time ago that letting a man get away with everything means you will soon be waving goodbye to him. You are not the friend who has known him since primary school and accepts him for who he is. And if he doesn't meet your standards; he has to go.

CHAPTER 33

IF IT SOUNDS TOO GOOD TO BE TRUE IT PROBABLY IS! BUT IS IT REALLY?

When your heart is breaking, and believe me, I know how much it is breaking, you may actually believe that the best and the quickest way to fix it is to call your ex and tell him how you feel. You may think that he will understand how you feel, proclaim that he feels exactly the same and the two of you will ride off together into the sunset. Well, sadly, even if he is actually feeling the same pain as you, it would be very unlikely for him to drop his guard and want to get back together instantly.

In my twenties, like many women all over the world, I was hooked on the *Sex And The City* series, where modern day women discussed things that had hardly been openly discussed in public, and certainly not on television before. When Carrie's relationship with commitment-phobe Mr. Big doesn't work out, she starts dating a handsome interior designer, Aidan, who is mature, knows what he's after (in this case - a committed relationship) and openly shows his affections and admiration for her - which she had fought for months to get from her ex-boyfriend. What does Carrie do? She behaves exactly the same way towards her new man as her ex was behaving towards her, later questioning herself. Do we need drama to make a relationship work? Do we have to endure tears, rejection and abandonment to be crazy about our partners, or does it just make us act crazy? And after much time thinking about the issue, Carrie proclaims: "When things or people come too easy, we become suspects."

I can't tell you how much this sentence struck a chord with me after my own break-up. It was like suddenly and finally everything I'd felt and experienced fell into place!

"When things come too easy, we become suspects." In other words, if something is too good to be true, it usually is just that: too good to be true.

This is the complete answer to the mystery of why millions of men all over the world can't appreciate a relationship with a good woman. If it came too easily and he didn't have to fight for it, it triggered feelings of suspicion. So what's next? Endless questions that he will start asking himself might include:

"Why does a woman like her (intelligent, good-looking, successful) want to be with me, not someone else?"

"Why did she so quickly become mine?"

"Why did I not have to flight for her?"

"Why was she even still single - surely men would kill to be with her?"

"Maybe there is a reason she was still single?"

"Maybe she is 'damaged goods', a complete bunny boiler or there's something else wrong with her she hasn't yet told me about?"

"Maybe she's desperate, needy and lonely?"

"Maybe she will want me to abandon my life, friends and hobbies?"

"Maybe, just maybe, she is not that special after all?"

When a man starts to come to these conclusions (and many other ones, because quite frankly the possibilities here are endless), it can only mean one thing for your relationship: he will now back off physically and emotionally, in other words - he will play hot and cold. And as he watches out for possible signs that his suspicions will be confirmed, you are going into rejected-crazy-abandoned-insecure mode where you demand more proof of his love. But you are actually playing right into his hands by providing him with all the evidence he needs to confirm that he was right.

And even if we know that this is utter nonsense - because you are worth ten of him - desperate, volatile behavior will not prove to him otherwise. I don't know about you, but I do not advocate playing of the dumb roles in a relationship, nor do I pretend I am someone I am not, and I am certainly not advising you to act in such way. But in order to be respected you need to understand how his mind works and then act accordingly.

When I think how easy it was for my ex to get me, maintain a relationship with me and have me at his beck and call, I am truly surprised that our relationship lasted as long as it did. Since apparently we only value things we've worked our asses off to get, he did not have to work very hard to be with me at all. If I asked you which pair of shoes in your wardrobe you value and look after the most - what would you say? Is it the cheap, easily replaceable pair from a local shopping center, or the exclusive pair with red soles you saved up for a year to buy? Likewise, would you put a protective sleeve on a cheap laptop, or would you only bother if it had set you back by a considerable amount?

The idea here is simple: we need to act as if we are a price for someone; an exclusive reward. And we can't just pretend that we feel this way, we really need to *believe* it is true, and this is the key to success with men. Having the strength and confidence to realize that you are a top prize for someone will be empowering enough to gain you new confidence, and ultimately an incredible amount of respect, which is exactly what you need to keep a man interested and hooked on you.

CHAPTER 34

YOUR ONLINE PRESENCE GOING FORWARD

In 2006, at Harvard, Mark Zuckerberg created Facebook as an online place for all his classmates to connect. Since then it has become open to over 400 million users. Owning and maintaining a Facebook account is free. But is it really?

I am not a massive fan of using Facebook for any other purpose than marketing. As I mentioned before, Facebook has only been around since 2006 and as far as I remember, when it comes to keeping in touch with people, we were doing fine before then. I'm not advising you to close your account, but perhaps you should consider the consequences of adding new people to your Facebook account too quickly. Like it or not ('like' being the operative word!), on this site we deliberately expose the most personal things about ourselves - from emotions to latest purchases - also telling people how we feel about others and ourselves. We express our opinion about millions of things that pop up in front of our eyes. It can be very powerful to build an image of yourself for others via Facebook by having hundreds of friends. But for a moment, go back and consider how overpowering and frightening it was when some time after your recent break-up, your trembling fingers were typing in your login details, terrified of seeing your ex wearing a new T-shirt (that you'd never seen), having fun on holiday with the lads, or even with a new woman. Remember how painful it was to see him proclaiming various things about himself and never mentioning you, like you never existed and he doesn't miss you. Learn from this; don't let it happen to you again. When you go into a new relationship, don't send your new man a friend request straight away. If he sends you one tell him you're not ready to take that step yet, which is perfectly acceptable, because neither he nor you should let each other into your lives too soon. You wouldn't do that in reality - so why do it in a virtual world?

Not becoming friends on Facebook with your new man has its advantages. You can't view his photos and read his posts, so you don't wonder whether that gorgeous blonde you spot in few of his photos is perhaps his ex-girlfriend. You can't flick through his timeline looking for details of his previous break-ups, meltdowns or work achievements - because quite frankly, his past is none of your business until he shares it with you in person. Seeing each other, especially in the early stages of a relationship should be enough for the two of you. Not befriending your man on Facebook also means that you remain slightly mysterious and more importantly - not completely available. How many times have you found yourself in the role of Facebook detective? Perhaps it's time to stop and maybe, just maybe, the new man will take much more interest in you and the roles will reverse – and because you are not too keen to provide all the information about yourself on a plate, you will finally experience curiosity from him, rather than the other way around.

Do I even have to mention that this also sends a man a powerful message that you are not massively interested in his life, are busy and contained within your own, and that he has to earn your respect first to infiltrate the circle of your closest friends or your whereabouts. And if the new relationship doesn't work out, well, the internet break-up is something you won't have to worry about at all! Not adding a new man to your Facebook friends means that you are taking preventative steps, thereby limiting the possibility of being hurt in the future by watching the parade of his life after you. We all suffer from a broken heart sometime in life, but going forward, it is only your responsibility to ensure that the damage is minimal and not deliberately repeated.

PART 7

THE END OF THIS BOOK, THE BEGINNING OF THE BRAND NEW YOU!

CHAPTER 35

LAST FEW WORDS FROM MAGDA

Every day of every week, millions of women go through the break-up of their relationships. Some learn from their mistakes and alter their ways, but some remain in the same pattern of behavior that has only brought them misery. Taking into consideration all that you have just been through and how difficult the journey back to 'normality' was, what choice will you make?

I wrote this book not tell anyone what they must do, but in a way that, I hope, will show that we all have choices to make in order to reach happiness. And I truly wish that you adapt some of the key thoughts into your life to help you understand your personal priorities. These thoughts reappear through the whole book, build on each other and gradually form a full circle of conclusions. The most significant thing for you right now though, is to shift your perception of what's really important. And 'that man', is certainly not important anymore!

The very first thing you should do after reading this book is to establish where you stand in this very moment your life. Be honest with yourself, only then will you truly know how and what you need to recover. Right now, while you are motivated, it is easy to get the ball rolling. Sometime later, when your boost of motivation might start running low, re-read some of the chapters, or all of the book, to get there again.

I wrote this book in Roses, Spain, after my return to Europe from America. I wrote it in three days. I thought about writing it on the plane crossing the Atlantic. But of course, I still had to return home to London two weeks later, where my previous relationship had started, finished and where my ex still lives and works. Did I worry that after all this time (a few months), the return home to the apartment where he had shared my bed and my time, would bring it all back? To be honest, it had crossed my mind on few occasions. And yes, I was worried. But the moment I touched down at London, Stansted, I just knew it wasn't going to happen. I'd triumphed over the pain and ultimately I'd won the best prize; my own self back. And I guess, and this is in no way false, I have to thank him for what he had put me through. I have a strong suspicion that it happened for a reason and maybe the universe wanted me to prepare myself for that special someone who may arrive in my life anytime soon. But more than anything, I know that I will NEVER make the same mistakes again!

And just as I was about to wrap this up, Pink's *'Try'* came on the radio

'Where there is desire

There is gonna be a flame

Where there is a flame

Someone's bound to get burned

But just because it burns

Doesn't mean you're gonna die

You've gotta get up and try, and try and try'

So, never give up trying! You will get there sooner than you think.

Magda

CHAPTER 36

HOW TO GET THE GUY: CAPTURE THE HEART OF MR RIGHT

Don't wait until the next time; don't wait until you're forced to wipe out tears whilst closing the door after another man has walked out. You deserve better then a man who simply doesn't respect you or doesn't appreciate you. Now is the time to ensure it won't happen to you again.

If you're tired of being dumped or repeating the same dating scenarios, if you want to quit obsessing why he 'needed space' or why he suddenly went cold and started ignoring you, you need to learn about dating and relationships. In my book 'How To Get The Guy: Capture The Heart Of Mr. Right', I reveal what makes men instantly attracted to women of ALL ages and backgrounds.

In the last five years, through writing my books and further contact with my readers, I have gained unparalleled access into the mistakes women make whilst meeting and dating guys. With this book I address the most notorious 'man trouble' and share the dating secrets that make guys chase women and commit to them. I will answer the most important questions about forming and staying in relationships and reveal the depths of female power. Along the way, I will explore the urge to chase after the proverbial bad boys or emotionally unavailable men. I will share my strategies on how to free yourself from 'love addiction' and offer real solutions to destructive relationship patterns. With this step-by-step program, I will provide you with an alternative to disappointment, heartbreak, tears, loneliness and desperation by showing you how to take control of your life and help you meet your destiny TODAY.

If you enjoyed 'The Break-up Bible', you know that you can trust me to know both female and male mind. Whether you just want to know how to get another boyfriend, or how to turn around an unfulfilling relationship, join me on this essential journey to understanding how to attract and keep a partner, all packed into just over a hundred pages of an amazingly enlightening read.

'How To Get The Guy: Capture The Heart Of Mr. Right' is available as an Ebook from Amazon.

OTHER BOOKS BY MAGDA B BRAJER

What Smart Women Know About The Chase: The Practical Guide To Pursuing And Being Pursued

Some of us like to chase after men, others can't imagine ever pursuing a guy. But who will end up happier? The ones who chase, or the ones who don't? And what are the consequences of both behaviors? My book answers questions such as:

Why do some men skip the chase, even if they like a woman?

Why do they wait for the girl to make that first move or try to game her into it?

Will he respect you after he's taken what you've offered him on a plate?

When is the time to put a stop to pursuing a man, and let him pursue you?

What should a courtship look like?

How to behave to be valued and attract a proper

suitor?

The answers to all these questions, and many more, can be found in this very Ebook. Available to purchase from Amazon.

The Break-Up Bible 2: The Path Forward

What can you expect of The Break-up Bible 2?

BB2 will make you face life-changing questions like: *What do I live for? What are my fears? Will I ever love again?*

It will help you find solutions to problems like: *How can I achieve closure? What is draining my energy? How can I get rid of my anger about the break-up?*

It will encourage you to analyze issues like: *Why did I let him make me act so crazy? Can I now accept my part in our break-up? How can I improve my behavior in the future?*

So grab a notebook and pen, and join me on a very necessary and brilliantly positive journey on the path forward …

Available to purchase as an Ebook from Amazon.

Make A Sales Pitch For That Man: 5 Easy To Use Strategies To Lock His Heart Body And Soul Into Brand You

5 strategies to help any woman get the man of her dreams acquired during a week spent in an investment brokerage.

5 unique tools to transform your love life.

Specific words to help you bring him closer and get him hooked on you.

Innovative negotiating skills that will get you what you want.

The resources and turnaround tools to reverse lack of attention, interest and commitment.

There is no BS here, just a short and powerful messages that will work on ANY MAN and change the way you behave and act around men forever!

Available to purchase as an Ebook from Amazon.

It Really Is All His Fault: What Would Push An Intelligent And Successful Woman To Behaviours She Didn't Even Know She Was Capable Of?

Is your life plagued by immature men with massive commitment issues? Or emotionally unavailable, who simply disappear when you need them the most? Then read on!

Do you find it hard to communicate with your man?

Perhaps the chronic arguments are killing your relationship?

Have you ever found yourself furiously dialing his number, only to be ignored, which fueled your rage, made you feel miserable and wanting to do it even more?

Have you ever been disliked by his friends because of your "psycho" behavior?

Do you find that despite your best efforts to resolve arguments and conflicts – your partner repeatedly blames you for the problems?

Do you need reassurance that you're not alone?

Then read "It Really Is All His Fault". Magda B. Brajer engages in the case studies about women who are driven mad by their men AND then get blamed for acting crazy. Join her on the journey of female sanity. You will be glad you did so!

Available as an Ebook from Amazon.

ABOUT THE AUTHOR

Magda B. Brajer is an internationally published author, who, through her inspirational books helps her female readers heal, reach their emotional goals and change their lives.

Magda is best known for "The Break-up Bible: The Keep Strong, Let Go And Move On Guide" and its sequel "The Break-Up Bible 2: The Path Forward", Ebooks she has successfully self-published in over 170 countries.

Magda currently lives in North London and is working on variety of new projects, including a romantic novel and series of novels for children.

Visit Magda's website:

www.magdabbrajer.com